.

ALL RISE!

A Conversation with
Judge Barbara H. Caldwell

Other publications by the Author
ABOUT MY FATHER'S BUSINESS, THE *Wisdom of Mose Jones*, published 2006 by Father's Voice Publishing, LLC, Marietta, Georgia. ISBN 13978-1-60145-092-0

BUSINESS LAW HANDBOOK, Understanding the Big Six, published 2007 by Kendall / Hunt Publishing Company, Dubuque, Iowa. ISBN 978-0-7575-4517-7

For speaking engagements, book orders, and interviews, contact Publisher:

Father's Voice Publishing, LLC
PMB Number 757
1480 Terrell Mill Rd. Ste. F
Marietta, Georgia 30067
678-467-4822
www.advocatesofchrist.org

ALL RISE!

A Conversation with
Judge Barbara H. Caldwell

Frederick D. Jones
with Lucinda Perry

Table of Contents

Preface

This book has been written to demonstrate and encourage Christian judges, lawyers, educators and all professionals to use our platforms, positions and titles for the furtherance of the gospel of Jesus Christ.

St. Francis of Assisi, founder of the Franciscan order, 1181-1226 said, "Preach the Gospel at all times, and when necessary use words."

This work is based on a one-on-one, straight from the heart interview with the Honorable Barbara H. Caldwell. Also included are recent speeches, prayers, a study and reflection section following various chapters.

We believe that this manuscript will touch all people of all ages, both male and female. The student will find guidance, the parent will find wisdom, adults will find inspiration, and all will find and feel integrity and character.

The use of this book as a Sunday school text, a personal devotional, seminar presentation or book club discussion is welcomed.

It is our hope that the reader will walk away inspired, uplifted and raised to a new level of consciousness regarding our role and responsibility to demonstrate the gospel through our practices.

"It is no use walking anywhere to preach unless our walking is our preaching."   St. Francis of Assisi

Introduction

December 4, 2005, we were planning our first "Evening with the Advocates" at the Georgian Club. The weather was bad. I was concerned about the attendance. I was scared to death that nobody would come because this was my first attempt at holding such an event at an upscale venue in Atlanta since starting the ministry. The weather was stormy, with hail and lightning. As I was meeting the attendees, I saw a lady sitting against the wall. I spoke with her and another lady and welcomed them. I had no idea at the time who she was and did not remember her name. Shortly before the program ended, this lady got up and left the event. Another attorney came to me and said, "Fred, that was Judge Barbara Caldwell from Douglas County, and you failed to acknowledge her." I was mortified that I had overlooked such an important official. Monday morning I found her name and court location on the Douglas County website. I zoomed to Douglas County to speak to this judge that I had so woefully ignored.

As I entered her office, the first thing that I noticed was that there was an open Bible on her desk. Her first words to me were, "To what do I owe this honor? I can't believe that you have come out here to see me. I never thought that you would be coming to visit me today." Her entire demeanor was one of a humble servant. We began to talk and there was an instant connection spiritually. The conversation flowed very easily. She said, "As we were preparing to leave home, it literally began to hail outside. I told the person I was traveling with, that I didn't know what we were going to, but it must be God. I got there to the meeting and I see this young man up there and I told my friend that this young man doesn't need anything from us." When she said that, I was thinking to myself, "If she only knew!" Judge Caldwell began to tell me that when she saw the name, *Advocates of Christ*, she decided that she wanted to know something about this organization, and that's why she came.

From that Monday morning, I feel that there has been a David and Jonathan connection between this judge and myself. The insight, the wisdom, and the encouragement that she distributes naturally have enabled me to move forward with a vision of the *Advocates of Christ* in a way that has made the organization more dynamic and vital in reaching the legal community. She is a woman of character, integrity, upright, authoritative, her yea is yea and her nay is nay.

These are the attributes that I believe God has called this organization to exhibit. Therefore, as I have gotten to know her over the last 3 years, I have seen her practice these principles over and over. Her counsel to me during some difficult personal times has simply been correct and on target. As a result, I believe it would be fitting to publish her life story such that others may read it and perhaps model it, as she is a living demonstration of an Advocate of Christ.

I attended one of the first "Just So You Will Know" meetings in Douglas County. Judge Caldwell narrated the program that evening. Young people in abundance were there asking questions to county government officials, and the community received information and feedback about the various services that the government provides. The mayor of Douglasville, a local radio personality, the sheriff of Douglas County, and other officials were in attendance and responding to questions. It was a high impact program, very informative; it provided young people with alternatives and showed people that government and law enforcement were concerned with their welfare.

On another occasion, I attended a Ladies Bible Study at the community center in Douglasville. I heard one after another of the ladies offer testimony about how Judge Caldwell had been an inspiration to her. One lady resigned her job to start a daycare center, her first love. Now her day care center is one of the most successful in the county, and Judge Caldwell was there to support her all along. Other ladies had lost their spouses, and there was Judge

Caldwell being a source of strength and inspiration. Other ladies had problems with their children in school and they needed someone to talk to; they found that in this Bible study. Another talked about divorce and how Judge Caldwell stepped into her life and just helped her maintain her sanity.

She emceed the Evening with the Advocates 2006. Her presence set a tone for the evening and the event that honored God and cultivated an atmosphere whereby lives were touched and changed by the Holy Spirit.

She has visited every school in Douglas County to read to the children, mentor struggling students, and speak to groups of students and parents.

She regularly meet with attorneys who are apart of the Advocates of Christ as a mentor and counselor providing a listening ear and a laugh over lunch.

Frederick D. Jones
The Advocates of Christ, Inc.
The Advocates Association, LLC

FOREWORD

In 1995, I was a new attorney in Douglasville. It wasn't long before I met Judge Barbara Caldwell. I remember first laying eyes on her and being in awe of how much she resembled someone who is dear to me, my godmother, who is deceased. That, alone, attracted me to her. As we talked, I immediately discovered other similarities that she and godmother shared; their compassion and love for life and others. Godmother was what the old folk called "good people." It was evident that Judge Caldwell was "good people" too. Almost instantaneously, I adored a woman that I had known less than one hour, not because she reminded me of my godmother, but because she was obviously a woman with pristine character.

Let me share with you, through my eyes, the characteristics of Judge Barbara Caldwell:

SHE IS A CHRISTIAN. The first thing that is apparent about Judge Caldwell is her Christianity. She is not shy about letting people know that she loves God. It is evident in the way she carries herself. Christ exudes from her when she talks and He is exhibited in her actions. She is a great example to those who want to know Christ and to those who strive to live a Christian life daily.

SHE IS HUMBLE. In the 12 years that I've known Judge Caldwell, she has consistently operated in humility. She has never treated herself as if she is above others. This is true even when she wears the robe. She doesn't consider the man who has great wealth and knowledge over the man that does not. She believes that every man has worth and treats everyone that crosses her path with dignity and respect. That's why people love her.

SHE IS LOVING. The Biblical scripture tells us there is no greater love than this, than a man lay down his life for his friend. Judge Caldwell loves people. She constantly gives much of herself and her time to the community and individuals, often before herself. She is "others minded." She always has others on her mind.

SHE IS TRUSTWORTHY. I could tell Judge Caldwell my deepest-darkest secrets and not be concerned about how she would respond or whether it would leave the room. How many people can you say that about? On the other hand, Judge Caldwell will tell you the truth. She tells you the truth because she loves you.

SHE IS AUTHENTIC. I don't know if you have ever met a "real person" or know what a "real person" is. A "real person" is down to earth. They don't measure themselves or circumstances against others. They walk quietly and never speak to be seen. A "real person" is flexible and can meet other people on their level. A "real person" has the ability to, as my pastor says, "walk with kings, but keep the common touch."

SHE IS AN INSTRUCTOR. Judge Caldwell takes to heart the Biblical scripture that speaks of God's people being destroyed because they lack knowledge. She has a heart for people to know, to gain knowledge. A former school teacher, she understands the importance of knowing. She realizes that people void of knowledge are prone to live defeated lives. She has made it her mission to educate whenever she can. She has a heart for young people to develop in knowledge and wisdom so that they can succeed in life.

SHE IS COMMITTED. One of the things I adore about Judge Caldwell is her commitment to the people in her life. As I interviewed her for this book, I discovered that her family and friends are very important to her. By the time I finished interviewing her, I knew that I was privileged to be among the number that she calls friends. But Judge Caldwell is more to me than just a friend; she is my big sister.

This book you hold in your hands is filled with 50 plus years of wisdom. It will inspire you. It will take you down memory lane. It will make you laugh; it may even make you cry, but in the end, you will know that it is a book filled with treasures.

Judge Barbara Caldwell is a gift to all of us; she is an Advocate of Jesus Christ.

Lucinda Perry, Esq.
Douglas County, Georgia

www.LucindaForYourRights.com

Nomination for Justice Robert Benham Community Service Award

Judge Barbara H. Caldwell is an outstanding example of an individual who combines a professional career with outstanding service and dedication to her community. Judge Caldwell would be a worthy recipient of the Justice Robert Benham Award for Community Service.

Judge Caldwell began her professional career in 1984 when she was appointed as Magistrate Court Judge for Douglas County. Judge Caldwell has served in that position for the past 23 years with dignity, authority, and sensitivity. She presides over first appearance hearings and pre-arrest warrant hearings, addresses civil and criminal complaints from citizens, issues arrest warrants, and performs wedding ceremonies as part of her professional duties. Her knowledge of the law and professional demeanor have earned her the respect of legal and law enforcement personnel, citizens of the county, and state officials as reflected in her numerous awards and recognitions.

Judge Caldwell takes her responsibility to her community seriously. She co-founded the well-known and popular "Just So You Will Know" annual community forum in Douglas County where citizens are invited to address various issues that concern them and receive responses from county officials. Her efforts on behalf of the citizens of her county have led to the resolution of a number of issues in the county.

Her love of the law and her legal profession is evident in her animated community service, her participation in professional organizations such as the Council of Magistrate Judges, and her eloquent words at any of her frequent invitations to speak at public gatherings. However, her passion is for serving women and children through her ministry of Christian counseling and Bible teaching. Inspired by her grandmother and her mother, both strong women who faced challenges with love and kindness, Judge Caldwell has dedicated her life to helping women find practical solutions to everyday problems. Judge Caldwell is the founder and driving force behind "Women in the Word" community-based Bible study groups and annual Christian fellowship retreat. Since founding the program in 1987, Judge Caldwell has reached women all over the metro area with her message of love, encouragement, determination, humility, and hope through faith in Christ. She directs the Bible study meetings, speaks to groups at churches and retreats. She organized a group cookbook project and completed two cookbooks, "Heavenly" and "Cooking for Love and Life" as fundraisers for the program. Her energy and enthusiasm for exhorting women to find Bible-based solutions to problems has contributed immeasurably to the improvement of those who are fortunate enough to be in her circle of influence.

Judge Caldwell is a proponent of lifelong learning and models her belief that education contributes to personal as well as community advancement. She is currently pursuing certification in counseling in order to expand her counseling services and assist more women in addressing their problems with hope through faith. The certification in counseling will open even more opportunities for her to serve the women of her community.

In 2006, The New Mountain Top Baptist Church in Winston, Georgia honored Judge Barbara H. Caldwell as one of the "Legends of West Metro" for her significant contributions to the well being of citizens in the Douglasville community. She lists this award at the top of her list of achievements on her resume, a clear indication that she values this recognition above all others. Certainly, it is most representative of her lifetime of service and dedication to the citizens of Douglas County.

CHAPTER ONE
Childhood

"Can a mother forget the baby at her breast and have no compassion on the child she has borne? Though she may forget, I will not forget you!"

Isaiah 49:15 (NIV)

Where are you from?

I was born in Douglas County, Georgia, to a young girl still in her teens who already had a two-year-old son and no husband. My life from my earliest days has been filled with evidence of God's love and provision for his children. My family was rich in all the things that matter – love, caring, compassion, dedication, and faith.

What is your first, most vivid memory?

My most vivid memory as a child is of my grandmother. My older brother and my mother and I lived with my grandmother before my mother married. My grandmother was my mother. My most vivid memory of her involves her love and her caring. She would take my brother and me for walks. We would walk up the dirt road and she would pick blackberries or strawberries. I can remember a summer like that. During the walks, my brother and I would pull rabbit tobacco; it was called chewing rabbit tobacco back then. It was a little bush that had a stem, and a long string ran from the stem. We'd peel off the string and chew it. If you chewed it long enough, it became chewing gum. We would do that while our grandmother picked berries.

My grandmother was just the typical grandmother that loved and cared. She had 14 children; two of them passed away early in life. I was raised with my mother's sisters. My mother's youngest sister is only about six years older than I am. I remember staying on the farm and we would go out in the fields and help pull the corn. We'd play under the porch. Those were good times.

My grandmother was a stickler for a clean yard. I remember we had to sweep the yard. We used brush brooms. We pulled sticks from certain bushes, tied them together and made a brush broom. We swept that dirt and it couldn't have any streaks in it. It had to be smooth. We lived in a wooden house. It had holes and patches and the typical things you find in an old wooden house. During the winter, we would sit around the fireplace at night. I remember the fire going out and putting sweet potatoes in the ashes and cooking them that way. My grandmother would cook the best biscuits and gravy in the mornings.

My grandmother was the most giving person I know. She would give you what she had. You never went to her house and left without something. She would give you the clothes off her back if you needed them. My grandmother would stand up for what was right. She worked hard. She was a loving person. She never complained. Now there are times I long to have a grandmother. Grandparents are important, no matter how old you are. For years I would go and sit with my great-aunt and listen to her stories from way back. I loved to hear her talk. That's why I go to nursing homes. That's one of my ministries. I really hate to see anybody mistreat senior citizens and children.

My grandmother was a beautiful lady. She died in her early 40s, probably of cancer, although back then we didn't know what it was. I was only 5 years old at the time, but I understood what death meant and I missed my grandmother terribly. After my grandmother died, my mother got married to my stepfather. That's when we moved away from the old farm house.

What do you remember about other family members?

Granddaddy was in the picture, but he was kind of withdrawn. He was a quiet person. He liked to sit in a corner and he oversaw everything. When he said something, you'd move. When he picked up the axe to cut wood, the boys would know to move. They knew what to do. When it was time to harvest, he was on it. He provided the best he could for the family. At night, he would sit in his chair. Nobody else would ever sit in his chair. He would sit and wouldn't say much. But whatever he said, that was it.

I was born during the time when you didn't go to the hospital. You had the midwife, the lady that came into the home and helped the mother with her baby. In fact, I didn't have a birth certificate. I was forty three years old when I got a birth certificate. When I enrolled in elementary school, nobody ever asked me for a birth certificate. The  only time someone asked me for a birth certificate was when I was going for legal guardianship for my nephew, Nicholas. We found out then that there was no record of my birth anywhere in Georgia. I never knew my biological father. My stepfather adopted me so that I could get a delayed birth certificate at forty three years old.

Tell me about your childhood, what things stand out in your mind?

I have three younger brothers, one older brother, and no sisters; I'm the only girl. Whenever my mother worked, I had to take care of them even when I was 11 and 12 years old. I was cooking and cleaning house because my mother had to work. I was my mother's right hand; she could depend on me. We were limited in our funds, but we didn't know it. My mother didn't have dresses to go to church, so she would borrow dresses from her older sisters to wear to church. We had "hand-me-downs" or she would make my dresses. I thought it was the best thing in the world when we could get something. When I got old enough to wear hose, if my mother had a pair that didn't have many runs in it, she would give them to me to wear. If I needed a slip, she would give the best one to me. My mother loved me, and she loves me even to this day.

 I'll never forget the time when we took pictures at school. I wanted to look nice and pretty and my mother let me borrow her pop bead necklace. I put the necklace on and it was the only thing that stood out in the picture. I thought that picture was the prettiest picture in the world and I still have it. It's so much about

my childhood that I remember and now I see the significance of it.

When she got married, she still worked and my stepfather always had jobs that took him away from home. He worked with a concrete company that built bridges throughout the state of Georgia, so he would be gone for long periods of time. My brothers were always a challenge because they were always getting into trouble and doing things that were wrong. They had their responsibilities, but they wouldn't do them. They'd just come in and mess up. I was always a tattletale because they wouldn't do what I said. I would tell on them because my mother held me responsible. That was the bad part about my childhood; I was blamed for everything. But my mother was a good mother and she did the best she could.

The other side of the story is that I was always outspoken. I was labeled as sassy because I tried to explain what happened, and you didn't explain what happened in those days. You were considered "talking back." I couldn't help it because it was just me. I got reprimanded a lot because of that. Now, I didn't get that many whippings, but I didn't do the kind of things to get whippings. I was labeled as a back-talker and sassy because I would defend myself, and that stuck with me. I became a person who was always on the defensive if I felt that someone was attacking me. That was because I never felt like anybody had my back, as we call it today. I always felt like I had to take care of myself, which has made me a strong woman. That's what brought me close to God.

How are you like your mother? How are you different?

Barbara with her mother

There are two aspects where I am like her. She works hard and is not afraid of work. She believes in having her own things and working for herself. I'm like her in that respect. I like to work too. I'd rather have my own. Even after I got married, I wanted to be independent. The second aspect is that my mother is a giving person. She likes to share. When you leave her house, it would be like you just went to the grocery store or clothing store. She would give you everything from meat to salt. She and my father never had much growing up, so when they were blessed by the Lord to work and obtain possessions, they were willing to share what they had. I'm like that. I like sharing and giving. I like sharing information. I love to share knowledge. If I find out how to get out of a mess, I want to tell somebody else how to get out of it. I want somebody else to know how good Jesus Christ is. I'm big on sharing information. The Bible says, "My people are destroyed for lack of knowledge." I don't want to be guilty of that.

I asked my mother once, "If you had life to do over, what would you do differently about your life?" She said, "I'd get an education." She once told me "Barbara Ann," there's no Ann in my name, but she said, "I wish I was like you." She said, "You're a strong woman and I wish I was like you."

Barbara's mother, Geneva

I'm not like my mother in that she is a little apprehensive. She likes to stay in the safety zone. I'm the kind of person that will stand up for me. My mother will not stand up for herself.

I knew from an early age, 3 or 4, that God was inside of me. It was different. I knew from an early age, but I didn't know how to make it come out. Whenever I think about Him, it gives me strength and everything works out for the good.

8

How have your dreams and goals changed from childhood to now?

My dreams and goals have changed throughout my life. Growing up, we didn't have a lot of material things that the world would consider valuable. But I thought they were valuable. We had food, clothing and shelter. Whenever someone gave me something, I thought it was great. We've never been materialistic. I'd rather find a bargain than pay $100 for a pair of shoes. If I go to a thrift store and buy the same shoe at $5.00, I feel great. That comes from my mother having taught us to accept anything that anyone gave us. She taught us to appreciate what we had and not spend our soul, spending all of our money, trying to be like the Joneses.

My dreams have come true and they are coming true. I'm just excited and amazed and waiting for what God is going to do next in my life. I'm serious. Because what God has for me is much better than what I can ever claim or choose for myself. God is making all of my heart's desires come true.

"Why Do I Exist?"

Father God, in the name of Jesus we thank You for this beautiful day. We thank You for the opportunity for prayer.
We love You; we praise and glorify You, for You alone are worthy. We ask Your forgiveness for the sins we've committed and for our failures to be thankful unto You and bless Your name.

In one typical day in America—93 died from guns; 16,000 were raped, mugged, or robbed; 274 babies were born exposed to illicit drugs; 2,478 children quit school; and 1,340 teenagers gave birth. Commuters wasted 216,000 hours in traffic jams; the U.S. sent 14.5 million tons of carbon dioxide into the air; the national debt increased by $1.4 billion; Washington paid $80 million to foreign creditors in interest on the debt; 355 U.S. companies went belly up; and 5,500 Americans lost their jobs. (from U.S. News & World Report, June, 1991).

This is why I say like Paul in II Corinthians 5:20, man/woman's greatest need is to be reconciled to God. II Peter 3:9 tells us that God is not willing that any should perish (be lost), but that all should come to repentance.

So why do I exist?

This question can be answered adequately by God alone. We are assured that everything He has made, including man, was made for a particular reason.

"The Lord hath made all things for himself: yea even the wicked for the day of evil" (Prov. 16:4).

In view of God's creation of man, the answer to the question, "Why do I exist?" is "I am here to enjoy the earth, to know God, to do His will, and to enjoy Him forever." But when man rebelled against God....we became like sheep who have gone astray, each to his own way. When the first created people ignored God's purpose and pursued their own selfish goals, they set in motion the rebellious spirit that resides in all men and established the separation between God and man. That separation results in man placing his own purpose above God's purpose.

So, according to God, why do I exist?

1. I exist to know God.
John 17:3 *says "and this is life eternal, that they might know Thee, the only true God, and Jesus Christ, whom thou hast sent."*

2. I exist to know and fulfill God's perfect plan for my life.

Romans 12:2 says *"and be not conformed to this world, but be ye transformed by the renewing of your mind that ye may prove what is that good and acceptable and perfect will of God."*

3. I exist to be an agent for extending Christ's Kingdom.

What is Christ's Kingdom? Romans 14:17 *says "for the Kingdom of God is not meat and drink; but righteousness, peace and joy in the Holy Ghost."*

4. I exist to be made like Christ in character.

The Bible gives us the model for Christ-like character. *"But the fruit of the Spirit is love, joy, peace, patience, kindness, goodness, faithfulness, gentleness and self-control."* (Gal 5:22,23).

5. I exist to please God.

Read II Corinthians 5:9: *". . . wherefore we labor, that whether present or absent we may be accepted of Him."* *Scripture says "without faith it is impossible to please God."* (Heb. 11:6) and *"For it is by grace through faith that we are saved. . ."* Eph. 2:8.

6. I exist to reflect God's glory.

1 Peter 1:16 tells us, *"Because it is written, be ye holy for I am holy."* Holiness mean - being totally devoted or dedicated to God, set aside for His special use and set apart from sin and its influence. Matthew 5:48 says *"Be ye*

therefore perfect even as your Father which is in heaven is perfect."

7. My chief purpose in life is to glorify God. 1 Corinthians 10:31 says *"Whether, therefore, ye eat or drink or whatsoever ye do, do all to the glory of God."*

To glorify God is to appreciate Him, to adore Him, to love Him, and to subject myself to Him. My desire is that God be glorified in everything. We are here to glorify God in our bodies (1 Cor. 6:20). Whatsoever we do, eating or drinking or anything else, should be done to bring glory to God.

The church is not an entertainment center—we don't come here to enjoy ourselves, bring fried chicken and potato salad, attend programs, and participate in different groups. We come here to be trained to do the work of Christ.

Jesus says in Matthew 28:19-20, *"Go ye, therefore, and teach all nations, baptizing them in the name of the Father, and of the Son, and of the Holy Ghost; teaching them to observe all things whatsoever I have commanded you; and lo, I am with you always, even unto the end of the world."* That's not just for men. In the book of Joel 2:28-29, God said *"I will pour out my Spirit upon all flesh."* Ladies, that means us, too.

The average woman (according to a book called "The Pen Woman"), speaks 4,800 words a day and spends one year of her life on the telephone.

Now we may not be prophetesses like Anna, Deborah, and Miriam; church workers like Phoebe and Priscilla; queens like Ester; judge like Deborah; ideal mothers like Hannah; women chosen by God like Mary; housekeepers like Martha; female Evangelists like the Samaritan woman at the well; seamstresses like Dorcas; business women like Lydia; or preachers to the Jews like Anna; but we can all be what God created us to be if we seek, understand, and accept God's purpose for our lives.

Study and Reflection

DO I truly know God? Is He an important part of my everyday life? Have I accepted the sacrifice of Christ as personal payment for my sins?

DO I understand God's plan for my life? Have I taken time to study God's word, pray for guidance and insight, and then write down what I believe to be God's perfect plan for me?

WHAT have I done today to extend Christ's kingdom? Have I told someone that God loves them? Have I helped someone in need? Have I invited someone to study God's word with me?

IS God making me more like Christ every day? The process of creating something beautiful can be painful; it involves cutting off parts that don't fit, shaping, molding, pressing, and firing to create the perfect image. Can I find evidence in my life that God is working on me?

DOES my life please God? Do I trust Him wholly for every need I have in my life? Can I honestly say that I have handed over everything – children, spouse, finances, job, health—to Him for Him to control?

HOW do I reflect the glory of God to others? Do my words, actions and attitudes show that I hold God's holiness in my heart at all times?

CHAPTER TWO
Early Education

"I devoted myself to study and to explore by wisdom all that is done under heaven."

Ecclesiastes 1:13 (NIV)

Where did you go to school?

I attended Hutchinson Elementary School. The building that used to be the high school building is now Simpson Funeral Home. The elementary school was a house that stood down the hill from where the high school was. I remember going to first grade and getting off the bus, the big yellow school bus. I mean, that was the joy of my life, to go to school. My oldest brother and I got to go to school. There were only two rooms in this building for first graders. I was in one room and my brother was in the second grade at that time, in a different room. There was another first grade classroom on the other side of the building. I remember Ms. Eleanor Butler was my teacher. The teachers competed to get the smartest students in their class. I remember they used to have some kind of hard candy that was so good. They had to cut the candy because it was in a block. Ms. Butler would always bribe us with that candy. All of the children would run to her class because she had that candy. I don't know how they had it set up at the time, but I got in Ms. Butler's class.

We had a pot belly stove, and I can remember how it heated up the whole room in cold weather. When we got into trouble, Ms. Butler made us go sit by the stove and we would sweat and sweat. When it was cold we didn't mind, but when it wasn't cold it was our punishment.

I remember going to that big building that was the high school building for May Day. May Day was one day a year, in May, when everybody in the school would be out in the yard and we would have different games; we would have pop corn and hot dogs and other treats. Then we'd have a May Pole. A May Pole was a pole that sat in the middle of the school yard with strings hanging from it that looked like party streamers. Each person would have a different color streamer, and you stand in line and then go in and out, in and out, around the May Pole until you platted it all the way down. Ah, it was exciting. If you platted the prettiest May Pole, your class got the prize. It was a lot of fun. School is almost over and you're ready to get out. This was the school's treat for us.

What were your favorite subjects?

I liked all the subjects, but I really liked Social Studies and History. I was always challenged. The teachers called on me a lot. They could depend on me, but they knew I was competitive. The girl who was first was my best friend. We always competed. I just loved school and everything about it.

In those days we got promoted; we went to another grade. I got so excited when they gave us our report card at the end of the year and the teacher said, "You are promoted." The teacher would call you up to get your card. When I went to get my report card, the teacher said, "these are your A's and B's." I had all A's and one B! I was so happy.

My mother was proud of me. She never had to get on me about my grades. I loved to go to school. My brothers, though, she would always have to get on them about it. She might not have known a lot about what was going on, but she knew we needed an education. We had to help momma pick beans in the fields so that we would have money to buy clothes for school. Momma would take us to Atlanta, to Wells Fargo. We had only one outfit and we were so proud of that, to get to go to school. We looked forward to school.

We didn't get to go to school that much. During the harvest months we had to work picking cotton and beans. So when we did get to go, we were excited. School and church were reprieves for us. All the other times, we worked and stayed at home. Neighbors then didn't live close like they do today. Our neighbors were miles away, so we didn't see other people. It was a joy and a treat to be around other people. We were glad to go to school.

"Create in Me a Clean Heart"

Father, forgive us for losing sight of what is really important, and that is to know You. Please forgive us for ignoring You. We thank you for Your will and Your gifts and the purpose for which You made us. May today be the day that Your kingdom comes and Your will is done in us as it is in heaven.

The world is changing daily. In the blink of an eye, it seems, telephones have moved from hanging on the wall to hanging in our ears. Televisions have gone from black-and-white with rabbit ears to wall-sized displays in Technicolor. Plastic has become the substitute for currency. Things change so fast, it's hard to keep up. Every year, Beloit College in Wisconsin publishes a list of things that the current year's freshmen don't know or have never experienced. The list includes, among other things, –

The Soviet Union has never existed.

They have known only two presidents.

There has always been only one Germany.

They have never heard anyone actually "ring it up" on a cash register.

Smoking has never been permitted on U.S. airlines.

DNA fingerprinting has always been admissible evidence in court.

"Google" has always been a verb.
Diane Sawyer has always lived in Prime Time.
Bar codes have always been on everything.
Reality shows have always been on television.
They have rarely mailed anything using a stamp.
They have never put their money in a "Savings & Loan."
Disneyland has always been in Europe and Asia.
Acura, Lexus, and Infiniti have always been luxury cars of choice.
Television stations have never concluded the broadcast day with the national anthem.
Richard M. Daley has always been the mayor of Chicago.

The world is changing, but what we don't see is that the world's changes are not supposed to change us; we are supposed to change things. God gave man dominion over the earth to subdue the earth and all things in it. That means that we are supposed to be the agents for creating change in the world. The first step to creating change in the world is to ask God to change us. David said, "Create in me a clean heart, oh God, and renew a right spirit within me." Why does God want our hearts to be clean? We need to be clean for obedience, forgiveness, worship, and love. What dirties up your heart? Sin... *"For all have sinned..."*

Jesus told Peter, "Unless I wash you, you have no part of me." The washing of His disciples' feet represented the spiritual cleansing that comes with God's forgiveness of your sins. Unless you have experienced salvation, God cannot cleanse you and make you a part of His church. The first step to having a clean heart is to accept Jesus Christ as the Lord of your life and the Savior of your soul.

You know the story of King David, how he lusted after Bathsheba and sinned against God in order to have her. His sin started with his eyes when he saw her on the roof of the palace. His heart took what his eyes saw and turned it into an obsession that led him to do things that he knew were wrong. David didn't have a clean heart, he had a bad heart. But David realized his problem and cried out to God to replace his bad heart with a new one. In other words, there was nothing in David's heart that God could use. He didn't need a spot remover; he was not asking for reformation or restoration, he was asking for something brand new, created by God.

Consider Eve in the garden, her eyes saw the fruit - it was good to eat. Then her heart led her to disobey God by eating the fruit. Eve had a bad heart. The stories continue in our world today; politicians and entertainers and even preachers get in trouble because their hearts are not clean before God and they do things that are wrong.

Sometimes we hear the invitation; "Give your hand to the preacher, give God your heart." Now I ask you, what do you think God wants with that old, dirty, nasty heart of yours? He doesn't want it. He hasn't asked anybody for his heart.

He wants to give you a new one.

"Create in me a new heart" is what David is asking for. Paul said "For we are God's workmanship, created in Jesus Christ, unto good works, which God hath before ordained that we should walk in them" (Eph 2:10). Therefore, if any man be in Christ he is...what? A new man!

Are you praying for a clean heart, like David? Why do you need a clean heart?

First, you need a clean heart so that you can be obedient to God. David wasn't obedient, Eve wasn't obedient; their hearts led them to commit sin by disobeying God. If you are going to be of use to God, if you are going to be a true servant, you must have a clean heart.

You need a clean heart so that you can forgive. Mark said "if you hold anything against anyone, forgive him, so that your Father in heaven may forgive you your sins." Paul instructed the Colossians to forgive as the Lord forgave them. Forgiveness comes from having a right relationship with God.

You need a clean heart so that you can worship God. A dirty heart is selfish and self-centered. A dirty heart puts its own desires above everything else. If your own desires are the most important thing in your life, then you can't truly worship God as the Almighty Creator and Sustainer.

You need a clean heart so you can love God, love others, and love yourself. God says you need to love Him first. After that, you need to love one another. Well, it's impossible to love one another if you don't love yourself. And you can't love yourself if you don't love God because he is the one who created you. So loving God is the first step to all other love.

How can you have a clean heart? Through prayer; no man can create a clean heart for himself, only God can do that, and he'll only do that if you ask Him. You know the things in your heart that you aren't willing to give up, the strongholds that you lock up tight. You've got to deal with those by giving up the key to God, letting him come in and remove those things and set you free. Then he'll remove that old, dirty, nasty, sinful heart and create a brand new heart just for you.

"I need a new heart" David said. Do you need a clean heart? Then pray for one. God and the things of God are so different from the world and the things of the world.

People of the world say that prayer changes things. Not so. Prayer changes people.

Study and Reflection

READ Psalm 51 thoughtfully and prayerfully. What is David saying in this Psalm?

The first step to getting a clean heart is confession. In verses 1 through 6, David confesses his sins to God. "Against You only have I sinned and done what is evil in your sight." God doesn't need for David to tell him what his sins are, God already knows. But David needs to put his awareness of his own sin into words. What sins do you need to confess to God? You need to put into words those things in your heart that are contrary to God's purpose and will for your life.

David asks for God to remove all the impurities from his heart. Cleaning out the dirty things in your heart isn't easy, it can be painful. Hyssop is used to heal cuts and bruises, but it is astringent and bitter like Merthiolate. It is painful to be healed. David says that God has crushed his bones; he feels broken all the way through his body by his sin against God. Are you ready to withstand the pain of healing? Are you ready to ask God to remove those things from your heart that are keeping you from true worship and love?

Beginning in verse 10, David sees what a new, clean heart can do for him – he will find joy and sustenance, his tongue will sing of God's righteousness, and he will lead others to God. Do you have a vision of your life when you have a clean heart? How will your new, clean heart reflect in the things you say and do and think? How can you reach others with the wonderful message of God's love?

CHAPTER THREE
High School

"Since my youth, O God, you have taught me, and to this day I declare your marvelous deeds."

Psalm 71:17

As a teenager, did you have a favorite hangout?

We didn't have hangouts. School was our hang out. Of course, you had your crowd. My crowd in high school was the homely people. I wasn't the cheerleading-type person; we didn't have cheerleaders anyway, but then I wasn't one of the ones that dressed very nice and came from a rich family. Mine was the homely group. We stayed laid back. Among boys, I was always a favorite because my brothers taught me how to play basketball, baseball, football. I could talk their talk. Whenever we got together and the boys needed another player, they called me. Even when I got married, I was the only lady who would go with the men to the football games. My husband and I would always go to the games together. If the guys went with us, I was the only lady that went because I knew about football. I knew about baseball. My baby brother, Terry, played professional baseball, so I knew about the game. My stepdaddy loved baseball. Back then it was all about the Dodgers and the Giants; the Dodgers and Cardinals; the Dodgers and whoever. When they played the World Series, the families came from miles around to one house—whoever had the television -- and watched the game. That was something. We'd also watch Saturday night wrestling and boxing. That was a big thing. They'd fry fish. That was the best time.

Barbara Harper – high school

I never considered myself pretty or attractive at all. I had a big gap in my teeth in the front. I did not have pretty hair. I had pretty hair until I was five or six and then I got a disease in my head called eczema. My mother put anything she could think of on my head to keep that sore from spreading all over. She put so much stuff on it that my hair changed. So I never really had pretty hair. My hair was plaited most of the time until I got older. My cousins who were the same age I am had pretty, long hair. So I was always the plain one of the three. A math professor in high school once told me in reference to my teeth "Daughter, that's your personality. That's who you are." But I couldn't see it. I didn't have a boyfriend. I wasn't really interested in boys. I was interested in school and extra-curricular activities. There were boys that I looked at and wished they were my boyfriends, but I knew they were off limits. I could never attract them because they were city boys. Most of them lived in Douglasville; they didn't live in the country. They would always have the pretty girls.

Did you join any clubs in high school? What were your interests?

In high school, I was in the drama club and on the basketball team. My friend and I were selected, while in the eighth grade, to be on the varsity basketball team. We were tall. The school didn't have a junior team; we had only one team. We were outstanding in basketball. I got a lot of trophies. I got awards for basketball, science, and physical education. I was in the chorus, and I was the Student Council President. Believe it or not, in my senior year a music teacher organized a jazz band and I was the lead singer. I thought it was the greatest thing in the world. I remember wearing a blue dress when we performed at one of our senior nights. It was just great. This was one of our senior year activities which included the prom and commencement. I really enjoyed them. I was the salutatorian.

When did you first start driving?

I started driving in high school, in my junior year. We didn't have a car that you could take to test drive. Back then you had to take your own car with you. We had a neighbor; Howard was his name. I went with him to get my drivers' license. My oldest brother was a mechanic and he used to love to work on cars. He and my husband, who was my boyfriend in high school, taught me how to drive. They taught me how to drive a stick. I didn't get my first car until after I was married.

What do you remember most from those years?

One of the most memorable events in my life was my high school graduation. My graduating class was composed of 46 members. That was the biggest class ever for that school. When I graduated, it seemed like something happened; a new world, a new life opened up for me. We never looked that far in advance, we were so wrapped up in school.

Barbara's senior year

The only two places we could go were school and church. We weren't thinking ahead; we weren't thinking about what would happen after graduation. My high school graduation was a great event. We got to wear the cap and gown. That was a big thing. We got to walk down that isle. You left one world and walked into another. It was beautiful.

High school was the greatest years of my life. I loved high school. I found myself. I worked hard in my academics. I studied hard to get A's and B's. I was second in my class. I enjoyed the challenge, and I wanted to be the best. No one ever told me that I could be the best; I just saw it in myself and I believed it.

What did your school years teach you about life?

High school now doesn't teach about life, it teaches about books, information. When I was in high school, we learned about life; how to live. We only had two places that we went and we loved; that was church and school. That was family life. Graduation was a huge thing. Now, kids can care less. In high school, our teachers cared about you learning. They knew what the world was going to be like. They taught us about things other than what was in the books.

I'll never forget when my principal, John W. Stewart, called me to his office when I was a senior. He found out, through the grapevine, that Al and I were dating. He talked to me about "keeping my skirt down" and "don't let kissing lead to other things." I'm not kidding. I'll never forget that day. That's how much John W. Stewart cared for his students. Back then, very seldom did you hear of a young lady getting pregnant out of wedlock. When one did, she was so embarrassed. They wouldn't let you come to school then. It was just a taboo. We couldn't smoke, either.

When you got in trouble, your parents got a phone call to tell them about it. Parents didn't go to the school and jump on the teacher or Principal. You got a whipping because the teacher or Principal had to call your parent. My mother would always say, "You might not have done what they said, but you did something. Otherwise, they would not have called."

I had to always excel to get the attention that my relatives were giving my cousins. They may have been the prettiest, but they talked about how I got good grades. I worked hard to be the best, and I knew I could be the best because I saw it in my mother's eyes.

What advice would you give to high school students?

My advice to students would be to learn all you can and enjoy, because once you finish high school it'll never be the same. You'll go on your different ways. In high school, you enjoy simple things; less complicated things. When you get out of school into the world, you are bombarded with so may other complex things until you have too many choices. When you have a lot of choices and alternatives, sometimes you might choose the wrong one. On the other hand, it's good for you. You learn lessons. Sometimes you waste a lot of time trying to pick the right one. If you only had two, you'd have a better chance of picking the right one than if you had ten choices. High school should prepare you to make decisions because you are going to have to make them. Even if you make a decision not to make a decision, that is a decision.

"Remember God"
(To the 2006 Cotillion)

Let your light so shine before men, that they may see your good deeds and praise your Father in heaven.

Young people as you prepare to move on to another level in your life, there are so many words I would like to say to you...words that will protect and keep you out of harm's way...words that will comfort you when it seems you don't have a friend in the world and nobody cares...words that will supply your every need when you find yourself coming up short...and "Mama, I need" and "Daddy, I need" won't answer the phone.

Words to say when your personal character, your morality, your ethical standards are challenged and tested; your quest for a higher education is hindered, blocked, or even denied because of the color of your skin, the texture of your hair, your faith preference, your socio-economical background...don't fool yourself. Bigotry, racism, and prejudices are still alive and kicking. Man can change the laws but only God can change the hearts.

But the most important and hope-filled words I can say to you to help you get through life's challenges are...

"Remember God...don't forget God." Scripture says in Ecclesiastes 12:1 "Remember now thy Creator in the days of thy youth..."

Life is a series of choices and decisions. Each day, we make hundreds of decisions that can bring us close to God or deceive us into thinking we don't need God, we can make it alone. When we live according to the principles contained in God's Holy Word, we embark on an abundant and eternal life.

God has invested a lifetime in you. Make a Godly legacy out of it, a life lived and left behind that makes a difference. Don't allow the devil to cheat and rob you out of your blessings of good character, excellent morals, and your desire to get involved in community activities, or reap the benefits of a successful career that He has purposed for your life.

Getting involved with drugs will rob you, gangs will rob you, skipping class will rob you, and poor grades as a result of not spending enough time studying will definitely rob you. Moreover, too much time in jail or juvenile detention will rob you. Finally, getting involved in sexual relations before marriage will rob you.

Dare to be and remain different. Be like Daniel and the three Hebrew boys, Hananiah, Mishael and Azariah—you may know them as Shadrach, Meshach, and Abednego. God did not change their names, Nebuchadnezzar did. He changed their names but he couldn't change their character, and they didn't forget their training.

Be an independent thinker. Scripture says, "Be not conformed to this world, but be ye transformed by the renewing of your mind." The world will profile you. Sloppy clothes, tattoos, piercings all over your body, tight revealing clothes, cuts in your eyebrows, bandanas, etc. You will be profiled as gang bangers and hoochie mamas...and other names I care not to say.

Pull your pants up, button your blouses, keep your skirts down—if God had wanted you to wear pants down at your knees, He would have put your waistline down there.

Stay away from all that; don't get caught up in all that, not just because it's right or wrong but because of God in you who has set a higher standard for your life. You don't belong to this world, you belong to God, and you are just on loan to your parents to care for you. Know who you are in Christ. What's wrong with "Yes Ma'am" and "No ma'am," "Yes Sir" and "No Sir?" Some of us have destroyed the English language. What you say and how you say it makes a difference. I know it does in my court.

Your pastor, your instructors, the staff, and your parents have been used by God to make a spiritual impact on your life, one that is everlasting. I believe God has used the R.E.A.C.H. program to develop in you the type of character, morals, and ethics you need to help reform you. I admonish you to take every advantage of the many, many, many opportunities to advance your education. Too many people have suffered and even lost their lives to open the doors of the colleges and universities so you can walk in.

Every child is a priceless gift from the Creator. And with the Father's gift comes immense responsibility. As parents, friends of parents, aunts, uncles, and grandparents, we need to understand the critical importance of raising our children with Godly love and Godly discipline. When the government began to tell us how to discipline our children, our society went to the devil. We, as Christians, are commanded to care for our children...all of them, not just the ones that look like us...our children at home and those around the world. All children need our prayers.

Get involved in your community's activities. Many have marched in the streets so we would have the opportunity to vote. Don't let it be in vain. Check out our schools, attend community meetings whenever possible. Get to know your child's teachers and instructors. It makes a positive difference in what they think of you and your child. Some of us have allowed our holiness to cause us to withdraw and shy away from civic involvement. Others have organized themselves into political action groups. Still others have found themselves destined to show that in the hand of God, one life can make a difference, even without the guarantee of civil rights. You are looking at an example right now.

Let us live the life we preach about before our children. We can't drink and abuse drugs and tell them not to; it's wrong. We can't say don't gamble and play the lottery and we play bingo for money. It's not alright to dance to rock and rap music just as long as you call it "Christian rock" and throw Jesus' name in it. It's not alright to purchase oversized clothing for your children and write "Praise the Lord" across the front. The scriptures tell us to come out from among them. They also tell us not to get entangled with the affairs of this world and not to touch the unclean things.

Ask yourself, how do I measure up? Not in the eyes of the crowd but in the eyes of God, an Audience of One. What we must never forget is that we are first and foremost called to live before an Audience of One who is the designer of our lives.

Let this be an encouragement to all of us...let's use whatever talents, positions, popularity, or wealth we have been blessed with to tell a lost world that our King, our God is not dead, He's alive. And He's able...to keep me...

The best way to say thank you for the talents God has blessed you with is to use them.

CHAPTER FOUR
College

*Commit to the Lord whatever you do, and your **plans** will succeed.*

Proverbs 16:3

When you graduated from high school, did you have any goals?

At the time, careers were never brought up. We just enjoyed going to school.

When I graduated from high school I really didn't have the kind of counseling I wish now I had had. When I graduated, it was like, "You've got to come up with something." I always thought I wanted to be a nurse. Then I didn't want to be a nurse. Then I said I wanted to be a beautician. My mother did take me to get my hair done for Easter, whenever she could, so, I thought I wanted to be a beautician. But I didn't make any kind of preparations beyond high school. My mother was concerned with us finishing high school and after that she said we were on our own. Two weeks before I got out of high school my science teacher said "Young lady, you're going to school." I responded that my mother couldn't afford it. The teacher told me to fill out an application anyway because I was going to school somewhere. He gave me an application for Morris Brown College because that's where he went. Two weeks before I graduated, I filled the application out and was accepted. By that time, all of the scholarships were gone. I didn't have any money, but I got in on a grant. It was a semester by semester type of thing.

Before I filled out the application for Morris Brown, I was lackadaisical. I had already started going with my mother to clean houses. She had gotten me a job in Mableton. I would have to ride the bus and walk three or four blocks to the lady's house where I cleaned. She had children that were younger than I am. One time while I was cleaning the lady's house, her children were talking about my mother. Her youngest child called my mother Geneva. I got angry. That's the last time I went to clean somebody's house. That's when I decided I was going to school.

Tell me about your college years.

My college life wasn't that good. I didn't get to enjoy all of the amenities that they enjoyed in college because I had to work. My mother and father were not able to send me to school and give me money for extras. They were only able to help pay tuition, and I got grants. I stayed at home while I attended college. I traveled back and forth on the bus.

I worked in college. When I moved to Atlanta, I would stay with different relatives of my mother. In my junior year, I stayed the last semester on campus. That was because I worked three jobs to stay in school and pay my tuition. I still didn't make enough money to pay for my education. I was on my way out because I didn't have any money. I was packing to leave when Mr. Bell called me into his office. He told me that I had been offered another grant that kept me in school. I knew that if I left school, I would never come back. I just had a feeling. So I unpacked and stayed.

I picked the wrong major in school. I picked chemistry. It was so hard. I had an instructor who was German. I look back and think "What was I thinking?" Then I switched majors and I chose Education. My studies went a lot better after that.

I'll never forget...I was taking Home Economics. My teacher pulled me aside one day and told me that I was sick. And I was. I would go to class and work after school. Then I had a part time job with Grace Hamilton, a State Representative. I worked at her home. Then I would go back to school and work in the Student Union Building. I'd have to stay up at night to complete my school work.

Ms. Hamilton told me to go home and get some rest. So I did. I was so sick; I had bronchitis and didn't know it. My roommate would bring me tea. That was my first experience with bronchitis. But I made it.

I remember when I was in a marketing class and I designed this black and white evening gown that my mother wore when she was queen at Golden United Methodist Church. I designed that dress. I enjoyed that. I was really kind of good at that. During my senior year, I was recognized as Ms. Home Economics. That was a surprise. I was asked to become a Delta Sigma Theta but I didn't because I couldn't afford it. That's one thing that I regret, that I didn't get to join the sorority. I liked the sisterhood. At that time, fraternities were big.

Why wouldn't your mother let you transfer to Clark?

My mother is one that is always cautious. She's very cautious. They didn't have the money and Clark was a little more expensive than Morris Brown. Even though they weren't paying my tuition and living expenses, she always wanted me to stay where it was safe. My mother thought it was more prudent to just stay there. She just didn't want me to move because she thought it'd be easier to stay where I was.

What's your proudest moment?

The proudest moment of my life is graduating from Morris Brown College because I had had such a hard time. There were many days and moments when I didn't think that I would make it. I rode the bus at 5:00 a.m. to get to the college, and returned home 7:00 and 8:00 at night. I studied late; I had to work for my grades. I worked wherever I could find a job. I worked in the Student Union Building. I worked cleaning up houses. I got a part time job working in the Department in which I studied. It was difficult, but I had teachers that liked me and tried to help me.

Now, there were some times when I got to enjoy college, but it wasn't like high school. My proudest moment was when I got my degree. After I graduated from Morris Brown, I went on to the University of Georgia. It wasn't easy. Back in the seventies it wasn't easy to get in UGA. I was in classes where there may have been fifty students and two or three black students. I was in a class where I was the only black. So, there was a lot of pressure on us. But I did get my masters from UGA.

What do you know now that you wish you had known when you were young?

I wish I had known that I did not have to think of every thing; I did not have to worry about things; that I did not have to care about everything. If I had learned to cast my cares on the Lord and give him my problems, situations, and my questions; I would not have all these gray hairs in my head. [Laughter] I probably would have some, but I would not have as many as early. [Laughter] But I'm serious. I wish I had known how good God is and how rewarding, refreshing, thrilling and amazing and awesome God is...His Word; the power of God, all these things...If I had known all that, you could not have catch me. I would have studied harder and done more things in the Church. God knew all of that. He let me come of age in my own time.

"Dependence on God"

Father in heaven you have given me so much. The miracle of life and salvation is beyond my understanding. The people around me, especially spiritual leaders, are priceless. I thank you for their faithfulness. I know that without faith it is impossible to please you.

Forgive me for losing sight of what is really important and that is to know you. Please forgive me for ignoring you. Your will and your gifts have taught me the purpose for which you made me. May today be the day that your kingdom comes and your will is done in me as it is in heaven.

When God gives me a clear determination of His will for me, all my striving to maintain that relationship by some particular method is completely unnecessary. All that is required is to live a natural life of absolute dependence on Jesus Christ. I must never try to live my life with God in any other way than His way. And His way means absolute devotion to Him. Showing no concern for the uncertainties that lie ahead is the secret of walking with Jesus. "You do not want to leave too, do you?" Jesus asked the Twelve (John 6:67).

To be born again of the Spirit of God means that I must first be willing to let go of the old things. Then I can grasp something else.

The first thing I must surrender is all of my pretenses or deceit. What my Lord wants me to present to Him is not my goodness, honesty, or my efforts to do better, but real solid sin, my sin. But I must surrender all pretense that I am anything, and give up all my claims of even being worthy of God's consideration. A self-assured saint is of no value to God.

I must surrender control over the direction of my life. Living a life of faith means never knowing where you are being led. But it does mean loving and knowing and trusting the One who is leading. Faith is rooted in the knowing of a Person, and that Person is Jesus Christ.

Dependence on God requires me to be constantly ready for God. Readiness for God means that I am prepared to do the smallest thing or the largest thing—it makes no difference. Readiness means having a right relationship to God and having the knowledge of where I am. When God provides direction, I must be ready to follow his direction with all of my heart. Carelessness, like disobedience, is an insult to the Holy Spirit.

Study and Reflection

READ Luke 14:33.

There is no way you are going to be fulfilled trying to be something you are not. The only way you are going to live a productive life, feel good about yourself, and carry out your calling in life is to discover who you really are. Find out what God has built into you, the talents He has given you. Use those gifts for the Glory of God, to edify the Body of Christ, and you will be fulfilled.

God has given me certain abilities and talents that I consider my strengths. Those abilities are -
1.
2.
3.
4.
5.

How should I use my abilities and talents to glorify God and edify the body?

CHAPTER FIVE
Dating and Marriage

A wife of noble character who can find? She is worth far more than rubies. Her husband has full confidence in her and lacks nothing of value. She brings him good, not harm; all the days of her life...She gets up while it is still dark; she provides food for her family and portions for her servant girls.

Proverbs 31:10-12, 15

How did you meet your husband?

I met my husband Al in the eighth grade. His father drove the school bus that I rode and he would ride the bus sometimes as well. He graduated two years earlier than I did. I was a school patrolman on the bus that my father-in-law drove. In eighth grade my husband was 6' 5" and he was always on the basketball team. In the eighth grade they chose my friend, Doris Smith, and me to play on the varsity team. That's how I got to be around him a lot. I thought he was cute, but he wasn't paying me a bit of attention. I didn't have pretty hair. All of his sisters had beautiful hair. Their ancestors were Indian. His mother was a beautiful woman, outside and in.

We didn't start going out until senior year. We started hanging with each other on the bus, coming and going to basketball games. He asked me to the prom. I was happy but cautious because I learned that he was one of the in-crowd guys, one of the guys that could probable have any girl that they wanted. They had competitions going all of the time, how many girls they could get, and I was one of those girls they could get. But I didn't give up anything; I didn't play that. I remembered Mr. Stewart telling me to keep my dress down.

There were one or two guys in that group that tried to trick me into that and tried to make me think that they cared about me. But my mother and my father liked Al. He came from a good family and my parents knew them. He came from a big family. He has four sisters and he had three brothers.

While in high school, my husband and I broke up so many times. The next thing I know, we are back together again in college. Then we started dating more steadily. There was no marriage proposal or anything. It wasn't a "Do you want to marry me." It was "We're going to get married when I graduate." That's how it was. We couldn't get married on a Sunday because he played baseball, so we got married on a Saturday which happened to be my birthday. So Friday I got my job teaching, Saturday was my birthday and we got married. Sunday we had to go to a baseball game because he played baseball with a team called the Pros. All of that happened on a weekend. My birthday and my anniversary are on the same day. That's something one should never do because you only get one gift. "This is for your birthday and anniversary," they say. I got married when I was 22. Back then, we thought 22 was old because most of the people in my class got married earlier than that. My mother and I were determined that I would graduate before I married. I graduated in May and got married in August.

My wedding was small. I made my wedding dress. I had $75 to put into my wedding. I bought the refreshments and two green plants. I don't regret it at all. The dress was white. It had a veil. It was a short dress, just below the knees. My Matron of Honor had on a pea green dress. It was cute. My daughters laugh at me when I tell them I got married on $75. Al and I had dinner at the old Rialto in Atlanta. We went to a movie and then had dinner. We thought that was big time. That was our honeymoon. We ate whatever we wanted. We were used to eating cheeseburgers, so it was a special evening.

What was the first big purchase you made with your spouse?

Our home was our first major purchase. It was a mobile home. I don't know how much the ring that he got me cost, but this is the band [looking at her finger]. I still have the band. The ring was small, but this is the diamond [again, looking at finger] that came out of the ring. It had a diamond. I still wear mine.

What makes your spouse special or unique?

At the time when we got married, we pretty much liked the same things such as baseball and basketball. We just had a lot in common. When he played baseball, I would be the biggest cheerleader he had. We were a couple that really cared for each other. We thought alike. He doesn't put a lot of pressure on me, and I don't put a lot of pressure on him. He lets me be me and I let him be him. God is in our marriage. He is the one that put us together. I look back when we were dating...we thank the Lord for keeping us together and helping us to wait until we got married and do things in the proper order.

My husband came from a country family like I did, and that's why my parents were crazy about him. We shared the same values. There's nothing like a good old country boy. You know what you got. Of course, he wasn't bad to look at either. I was never insecure with other girls and women trying to get his attention. It didn't bother me. I knew who I was and he knew who he was. He knew it was cheaper to keep me. [Laugher] I'm just teasing. He knew that I would be there. That was one thing I was never worried about. I always believed that you can't make anybody love you. I had a lot of people trying to tell me things about my husband that I wouldn't allow them to tell me. People would even write letters to my house. People told my mother things; that they saw my husband doing. I would tell my mother that I don't listen to the talk, and that people bring garbage, but I'm not a garbage can. I never played into that. I didn't have time for it. I figured if he wanted to go, what could I do about it. You think I'm going to worry myself over somebody that doesn't want me? If you don't want me, fine; somebody else does.

What kind of things bring you pleasure?

 I get more pleasure from intangible things. I don't think it's much different from when I was younger. I like to walk in the woods. I like picnics. Every family event brings me pleasure more now than when I was younger. Being with my husband

57

and children; us eating together, laughing together, going out together, going on vacations together brings me more pleasure more than anything I did when I was younger. I see the importance of family; being with them, knowing that they're okay, that they're in good health. That gives me more pleasure than anything else. There are no material things that can compare to that. Hearing them laugh, talking to them, spending time with them, that's wonderful.

"Building a Strong Christian Family"

The first and most important responsibility for a parent is to build a family that is strong in faith, strong in the love of the Lord and willing to live for Him. As parents, we have to consciously and deliberately train up our children in the ways of the Lord. If we start when children are small, faith becomes a part of their lives, but even if your children are older, you can start now to teach them the values that Jesus told us to hold.

To have a Christian home and family, you must first establish whom you will serve. There are two forces in the world—God and Satan. It seems obvious, but you must choose God. That means you must be born again. Joshua 24:15 says, "Choose for yourselves this day whom you will serve . . . but as for me and my house, we will serve the Lord."

I know that some of us come from or are in what we call dysfunctional families. Whatever family you are in, it is the right family, because that's where God put you, so work where you are. God has a purpose for your family. Genesis 12:3 "I will bless those who bless you, and curse those who curse you: and in you all the families of the earth shall be blessed." It's not too late, you can still build a strong Christian family if you work at it. Let's consider a few of the building blocks.

1. **Commitment.** Do not abandon your family—be there for each other. You may be the only one who is saved, but your example and your prayers and your persistence can change those around you, those who see you every day.

2. **Appreciation.** Thank God for each other. Express appreciation for each other – thank each other – encourage – share. Teach your children Exodus 20:12 – the first Commandment with promise. "Honor your father and mother." That means they must obey you, but out of respect, not fear. Teach them respect by example – doing so will be a great lesson to your children. As they learn to honor and respect authority, they will learn to honor God as their ultimate authority.

3. **Communication.** Every person needs to know that he or she is a part of a whole. It gives us a sense of belonging and security. It helps solve problems and resolve conflicts. Don't carry a grudge all your life, you need to talk about it and get it resolved.

4. **Spend time together.** Members of strong families spend time together, praying, working, having fun or just hanging out together. Families need large quantities of

good quality time. You may have to make time by giving up other things, but it's worth it.

5. **Ability to cope with stress and crises.** Don't forget where you are; even though you may have a strong family, you still live in a real world. During crises you must pull together. Strong families call on their commitment of each other and their good communication skills to help them work out ways to get through their difficulties. They manage to see some good in the situations—no matter how bleak they may be. The Bible says "Give thanks in all things," for this is the will of God for us. It's hard to remember sometimes that all things work together for good, but that's the promise that will get you through the toughest times. To do that, you have to trust God. Acknowledge that He is in charge and He's guiding your path, even when you can't see it.

When you are facing a crisis, seek a word from the Lord first. Then start to praise God for what he's going to do to bring you through this tough time. Praise is not just for worship on Sunday, it's for fighting; 2 Chronicles 20 tells us ". . . it breaks the bonds" of evil.

6. **Spiritual well-being.** Jesus talked about the importance of building our "house" on the right foundation (Matthew 7:24-25). Spiritual foundation gives meaning and purpose to life. In Christ there is hope, in

Christ we can free ourselves from anxiety, guilt, fear, and low self-esteem. He that the Son sets free is free indeed.

Families with strong spiritual well-being know that God is there watching, caring, loving etc. For He hath said, I will never leave...Put these scriptures in action. Be a doer of the Word, not just a hearer.

After you have taught your children as the Bible has instructed, stand back and see the salvation of the Lord. His word will not return void, God always keeps His promises.

Study and Reflection

Sunday is a special present from God to man. How man, and especially a family, observes Sabbath casts a great witness to the world. The principle in the Sabbath is that one day in seven should be dedicated to the Glory of God.

What has happened to the Lord's Day? It has become "Mothers Day," "Fathers Day," Dad's birthday, Aunt Susie's birthday, anybody else's birthday—whether it came last Wednesday, or will not come till next Thursday! Not only that—it is being used for Kid's Day, Dog Show Day, Hog Calling Day, Fishing Day, and Tour-the-Country Day. It is also Reunion, Wedding, Anniversary Day, the Day-

We-Get-Together Day, Make an Extra Buck Day, or Day-Off Day. It is easy to see why there is no more time for Christ on the Lord's Day.

He that loveth father or mother more than me is not worthy of me. Matt 10:34-39

How do I honor the Lord? Am I committed to keeping the Sabbath holy by avoiding things that distract me from the worship of Almighty God?

Starting today, I will commit to remove the following distractions from my observance of the Lord's Day.

1.

2.

3.

4.

5.

CHAPTER SIX
Early Jobs

"See then that ye walk circumspectly (with great concern for how you live) not as fools, but as wise, redeeming the time (making the most out of every opportunity) because the days are evil."

Eph. 5:15-16

How did you find your calling in life?

As I said before, in college I had no idea what I wanted to be.

I thought I wanted to be a Cosmetologist. Then I thought I wanted to be a Nurse. At one time I thought I was going to be a Chemist. After that I gave up and said "Lord, whatever." Then I remembered that I could teach.

I wanted to do something that I thought I would enjoy. I had enough credit courses in the area. I taught for nine years. That wasn't my first job though. One of the jobs I had in college was as a Dietician Assistant at St. Joseph Hospital in Atlanta. Ironically, the year I graduated my supervisor offered me a full-time position. I told the supervisor that I loved the job but that I had already been offered a teaching job at home. When I got the job on Friday I was Barbara Harper. On Saturday I got married. So when I went back to school on Monday I was Barbara Caldwell. From those days till now I can truly say my steps have been ordered by the Lord. I've been happy in every one of those steps.

I loved children and I loved teaching my class. When I first started teaching in junior high school, I taught my brother and my cousins. They were in my class. I had an Arts and Crafts class. It seemed to be about fifty of them in there. Most of them were boys and most had been repeaters. They threw me, a first year teacher, in there. My brother and cousins wouldn't call me Mrs. Caldwell. They called me teacher. They refused to call me Mrs. Caldwell and I would tell momma and my aunt. I said if I got through that year, I could teach anything. I love teaching.

What has been your biggest frustration?

The one frustration that I had in life was when I was not able to find a job. That was my worst frustration, because I loved to work. I knew that I was supposed to work; I wanted to work. So I had to find whatever job I could do.

When I was in college, that's when I had those different jobs. I remember one summer I got a door to door sales job so that I could make enough money to go back to school. I never forget when I took a job in Bremen, sewing flyers on pants at a men's suit company. I had a job downtown at Stouffers, cooking vegetables for the restaurant. I had to get up 5:00 in the morning to catch a bus downtown. Jobs like that were precious to me because they were the only kinds of jobs I could get back then. Whatever I could get, I would work. During the summer, it was hard for a black person to get a job. I couldn't get a job in Douglas County. If I got anything in Douglas County, it would be cleaning somebody's house. Of course, at that time I had quit cleaning houses. That's why I went to school. I did get a job working in the old mill in Douglas County, but that job didn't last but about two or three weeks.

If a young person came to you and asked you what's most important for living a good life, what would you say?

Finding and knowing yourself is most important. Know who you are and be content with it. Allow God to reveal to you who you are, because when God reveals to you who you are, you can excel; you can go anywhere and do anything. Be satisfied with who you are. A lot of people are trying to be like somebody else and they can't be happy.

You can't be happy trying to be somebody else. You've got to be yourself. God made you you for a reason. He didn't make you like anybody else and in that self there is success. God wants everybody to experience abundant life. I may not hit ten home runs, but I can bat. I can hit the ball. So I'm not a home run hitter; so what. That's not me. But accept yourself, and once you accept yourself, you can do and be anything that you want to be. Love yourself first. The first great commandment is to love the Lord your God with all your heart, body, mind, soul and strength. The second one is likened unto the first one; love your neighbor as yourself. If you don't love yourself, you can't learn to love anybody else. You've got to love yourself and know who you are.

"Spiritual Growth"

Question: Are you where you want to be? Are you with who you want to be with?

If the answer is "Yes,' then you ought to be happy.

We have a dual responsibility—to become the person God wants us to be in order to accomplish the purpose for which He created us. Think how tragic it will be to face Jesus for those who have failed to fulfill God's will and wasted their few short years only achieving material, social, and financial goals for self-gratification.

God is more concerned with who we are, rather then what we do for him.

How can we serve God? We can serve God by sharing His message, mercy, and love with those who cross our paths.

Everywhere we look, or so it seems, the needs are great; and at every turn, it seems are temptations. Still, our challenge is clear; we must love God, obey His commandments, trust His Son, and serve His children.

It is an encouragement that God takes care of those who serve Him by working through their imperfect decisions and actions. This is an example of what is called "Divine providence;" that is how God controls everything for his good purpose.

It's best to do behind the scenes, better not to let people know what you are doing.

Romans 15:4-5. Patience and encouragement comes from God.

For everything that was written in the past was written to teach us, so that through endurance and the encouragement of the Scriptures we might have hope.

May the God who gives endurance and encouragement give you a spirit of unity among yourselves as you follow Christ Jesus.

Romans 15:4-5 (NIV)

Spiritual growth takes place as we give not just material things, but what people need most: our love our forgiveness, and our understanding.

We daily live in the midst of many voices calling for our attention. We will always be tempted to satisfy our self-serving, fleshy desires. We also need to daily be on guard against allowing "good things," or even "good people," to occupy our time and keep us from the best God has for us. Life is far too short to allow material possessions and the desire for worldly accomplishments to dominate our lives.

The greatest competition of true devotion to Jesus is the service we do for Him. Are we more devoted to service than we are to Jesus Christ Himself? We are often so preoccupied with our successes and responsibilities that we are tempted to tell people what we are doing for the Lord, rather than what the Lord is doing in and through us.

Our opportunities to serve the Lord and to be prepared to meet Him will soon end.

"See then that ye walk circumspectly (with great concern for how you live) not as fools, but as wise, redeeming the time (making the most out of every opportunity) because the days are evil."

Eph. 5:15-16

Study and Reflection

To be surrendered to God is of more value than our personal holiness. Concern over our personal holiness causes us to focus our eyes on ourselves, and we become overly concerned about the way we walk and talk and look, out of fear of offending God.

There is no fear in love. But perfect love drives out fear, because fear has to do with punishment. The one who fears is not made perfect in love.

I John 4:18

We should quit asking ourselves, "am I of any use," and accept the truth that we really are not of much use to Him. –Mark 14:6

The issue is never of being of *use*, but of being of *value* to God Himself. Once we are totally surrendered to God, He will work through us all the time. Without surrender, our efforts will never have the outcome of bringing glory to God.

CHAPTER SEVEN
Career

He appointed judges in the land, in each of the fortified cities of Judah. He told them, "Consider carefully what you do, because you are not judging for man but for the Lord, who is with you whenever you give a verdict. Now let the fear of the Lord be upon you. Judge carefully, for with the Lord our God there is no injustice or partiality or bribery."

II Chronicles 19:5-7

How did you transition from a teacher to becoming a judge?

I was appointed Magistrate Judge on October 20th, 1984. I have served 22 years and I'm into my 23rd year. My first two years were part time and the last twenty years have been full time.

I had no aspiration of ever becoming a judge or anything in the judicial system or anything in government, period. I was minding my own business. I was working as a Director of Education at a local bank. In 1983 they changed the law from Justice of the Peace to Magistrate Judge. In 1984 every County was required to have a Small

Claims Court and Magistrate Judge. I can credit Leonard Danley for thinking of me. He came to me when I was working at the bank and said, "Barbara, we need you to be a Magistrate. Steve Messenger is looking for a Magistrate and now is the perfect time to get you in there." I didn't know anything about government. I went and talked to my pastor first. He said "Go for it. You've got to do it because God is the one doing this." Then I talked to my mother and she told me to stay where I was. As I told you, my mother is a safe person. She didn't want me to venture out. She was always fearful of me getting into something that she thought I couldn't handle. But I'm a pioneer. I'm a trailblazer. I wanted to get out there and make a difference. I accepted the offer.

Before becoming a judge I didn't know what I wanted to do. I always had an aspiration to open an academy and teach faith based subjects. I always pictured having this academy where I could teach the Bible, plus Science and English. I always had a vision where the children would wear uniforms. I tried to work on that but God steered me in a different direction. He said "You can still have what you want but I'm going to do it in a different way." It is coming to pass now; I can't begin to tell you about it.

What's the most difficult thing that ever happened to you?

The most difficult thing I can remember is a job; that would be this job on the bench. When I first started, I was so blown out of the saddle. Two weeks after I was appointed I was on the bench. I was asked by Judge Baker to preside over Ordinance Court. I was appointed to be Magistrate and forgot that Ordinance Court was part of the Magistrate Court. I was the only full-time Magistrate and he asked me to preside because he had to go out of town on an emergency. I was so nervous and scared. This was prior to me going for my training. I had to sit in on other hearings in order to get the feel of it and get acclimated to it. I was afraid and perspired in places I didn't think you could sweat. I say perspired, but I sweated in places I didn't think you could sweat, and was so nervous. But I prayed and asked God to give me the wisdom to go through, because at that point, I believed it would make or break me, to see whether I could do this or not. I had already questioned myself, "what you got yourself into girl." I never had aspirations to be a judge, but I got through it.

So many people gave me compliments on how I presided and how I carried out the hearings. During that time, you sentenced in Ordinance Court and gave both fines and community service. I never will forget this guy was in there for littering in the County. His community service was to clean so many different roads and pick up trash. I lectured him on and on about beauty and cleanliness, and how we want our County to look nice. I think he wanted me to hush, stop preaching so that he could start his community service. I'll never forget that. That was a turning point in my life.

My experience as a new Magistrate was so closely related to the first week that I taught school. I remember being nervous then. The first class that I had was 95 percent repeaters for the second and third time. It was elementary school. My cousin and brother were in there and the majority of the class was boys. Here I am teaching Arts and Crafts. I never took any courses in drawing. But you had to teach yourself so that you could teach the children. I had children I had to take to the office every day. Back then, you could paddle children. I would get the coaches next door to come and paddle the boys. They were unruly, disrespectful to me because I was a first year teacher. I had just gotten married; the Saturday before I started teaching school on Monday. There again, I made it through that.

That's what made me love teaching. I said if I could get through this year, I could teach anybody. That is true. Now I feel like I can teach anybody, because I love teaching. Now I feel like I can preside, because it's not so much about presiding, it's about being in control, but relating. I think you've got to be what you do. It's not just something that I'm doing by numbers and statistics...we are dealing with people and it's got to be relevant to life. You can't be going through the motion. I don't want that person back before me for any reason. So, I want to impress upon them the importance of doing what they're suppose to do so they won't have to come back to court. We don't want the person to be a repeater and not learn anything. We don't want to just correct the situation, but make the person a better individual so that they will know that they don't have to do that. We don't want error in our lives, we want truth. I guess that comes from my teaching; wanting to teach people and wanting to share information; wanting to make the person a better individual.

If you live another 20 or 30 years, what do you see yourself doing?

I see myself doing whatever the Lord has for me to do. I see myself working in the ministry of God. I love relating to people and trying to lead people to God. I'd love to be doing his work, in whatever capacity he wants me to work. It's enjoyable. I don't have to work as hard as some people that don't know the Lord. He puts things in your way. He fixes things for you. He provides a covering; he provides everything that you need.

What do you see as your place or purpose in life? How did you come to that conclusion?

When I gave my life to Jesus Christ, I found out that my purpose was to do His will; to be a witness for him, in everything that I do and everywhere that I am. I have to let my light shine before men that they may see my good works. Why, because I want God to receive the glory. My purpose is his will; to be a witness and I'm happy with doing that. Wherever he places me, what ever he would have me to do, then that's what I want to do.

"Guilty or Not?"

THOUGHT – Romans 2:16

This will take place on the day when God will judge men's secrets through Jesus Christ, as my gospel declares.

WORD – Matthew 12:36

But I tell you that men will have to give account on the Day of Judgment for every careless word they have spoken.

DEED – Revelation 20:12

And I saw the dead, great and small, standing before the throne, and books were opened. Another book was opened, which is the book of life. The dead were judged according to what they had done as recorded in the books.

I've been asked what title is proper for one to use to introduce me at Church gatherings. I always say "as a child of God" is alright with me. However, it is also proper to say Sister Barbara Caldwell, Judge Magistrate Court

Douglas County. Most of the time, the world honors you because of your position and or title and are proud to say so. I suppose this is one way they can identify with someone they think is important.

The world delights in saying "Oh! She's a black judge, he's a black attorney, or a black lady doctor or a black doctor" and are proud for the most part. Sometimes they are jealous for the lesser part.

But when it comes to the church, it's not about titles, positions, status; it's not about you, or me, or even Pastor. It's about Jesus Christ. Whatever you are is because of Jesus. And we should never forget to give all the honor, glory, and praise, because it belongs to Him and Him alone.

Most of the time speakers say, "I'm not going to be long today 'cause I know you have other places to go." But I say, "I'll be here about an hour or two" and you will say, "Yeah, and you'll be here by yourself." Especially in the black church, you'll go tipping out on me with your finger up in the air.

I have a question for you to consider today—If you were arrested for being a Christian, would there be enough evidence to convict you? I want to spend a few minutes talking about guilty or not!

What identifies a Christian? Most people would say a Christian is someone who attends Church; says he's a Christian because he or she joined the Church; someone who sings in the choir or serves on the usher's board or has some other position in the church. That may be enough to get you arrested, but how about a conviction? There has to be enough evidence for the jury to convict you. As Christians we are on trial, but our desire is to be found guilty! What would it take to convict you or me or your pastor?

In any legal case, there are elements of the law that have to be present in order to have an arrest and a conviction. Officers of the law and prosecuting attorneys must provide information concerning "who," "what," "when," "where" and "how" in order to obtain a conviction. How do those elements relate to being a Christian?

Who? Let's get a definition of a Christian – Baker's Bible Study Guide says, "A Christian is one who has understood the A-B-C's of the gospel of Christ and has taken his stand upon Him and experiences Salvation though Him." Let's simplify that even further; how about "who-so-ever" will, let him come – John 3:16 – Romans 10:13... who-so-ever shall call upon the name.... To sum it up H-B-O. I'm not talking about the cable channel; I'm talking about the H-B-O of life and death. Who-so-ever will HEAR the gospel,

BELIEVE the gospel, and OBEY the gospel, the same shall be saved.

What? What is a Christian supposed to do? First, be a witness, Isaiah 43:10 - "Ye are my witnesses, saith the Lord, and my servant whom I have chosen." Do the work of the ministry—preach the truth, teach, reach the lost, etc. Just look at the Church Covenant; that's what we are supposed to be doing.

When? All the time; not just on Sunday or Bible study night, every day we must take up our cross daily. If you are awakened at night, you should go to preaching. Anytime and anywhere, we should be ready to give an answer for the hope that is in us. Remember, you don't belong to yourself; you've been bought with a price. Always look for an opportunity.

Where? Christianity starts in the heart. Remember the words of the hymn – Lord; I want to be a Christian in my heart. Christianity is lived out in the home, with quiet time, family devotions, training your children, letting them know who the parent is and who the children are. We are Christians on the job. Are you ashamed to let people at work know you are a Christian? How about in your Church? Do you only act like a Christian when the TV cameras come on, raising your hands in praise or bowing your head in prayer?

How? By the power of the Holy Spirit ("without Me, ye can do nothing"). By knowledge of God's word – we must study God's word daily and commit it to memory so it becomes a part of the way we think. It's not just about being able to quote scriptures. I'm talking about living the word. "Put on the whole armor of God".... How do you do that? By faith!

"Ye shall know them by their fruits."

With this the prosecution rests.

Once the prosecution presents the evidence, the defense has an opportunity to challenge the evidence. Who would the defense call to testify against you? Your husband? Your wife? Your children? Your neighbor? Your co-worker? The mailman? Cashiers at the grocery store? Tellers at the bank? How about your pastor? What could others say against you to discredit your claim of Christianity?

How would you testify for yourself? "Though He slay me, yet will I trust Him. If I perish, let me perish; I'm going to see the King." "Lord, here am I; send me."

CHAPTER EIGHT
Children

As arrows are in the hand of a mighty man; so are children of the youth.

Psalm 127:4

How many children do you have? When were they born?

I have two daughters. Jennifer was born in 1973. She'll be 34 this year. Jessica was born in 1978. She'll be 29 this year.

What do you remember special about your children?

They are as different as night and day. My pregnancy with Jennifer was smooth, no problem. Everything went fine until delivery, but labor was rough, terrible; 30 plus hours of labor. I wouldn't dilate and they couldn't give me any kind of pain killers. Jennifer was born with a broken collar bone. At that time, they used forceps, and that damaged her. That's how difficult it was. Al was there with me and I believe I almost broke his arms. The pain was excruciating.

After Jennifer, we decided to change doctors. It took me five years to get pregnant in the first place. After that, it took me five more years to get Jessica. Jessica's pregnancy was terrible from day one. I had aches, pains, nausea. I had never had one day of nausea with Jennifer. We thought it was a boy because everything was different from when I was pregnant with Jennifer. Her delivery was hard, too. After Jessica was born, the doctor told me I couldn't have any more children; otherwise, it might be detrimental to me or the child. I wanted more children and I wanted a boy. Before Jennifer was born, I had a miscarriage. I believe we caused it because we were moving heavy furniture around, but I didn't know I was pregnant. I hated that because I imagined that was my boy.

My brother had a son named Nicholas out of wedlock. His mother, a crack addict, ran off and left Nicholas with a babysitter, and the babysitter called Butch, my brother, to come pick him up. At nine months he had bronchitis and was near death. My mother cared for Nicholas for a couple of months, but she was not able to care for a small child. So I took him in. He became my son.

Nicholas had problems. He got thrown out of one nursery at nine months because he bit a number of children. I put him in Kinder Care because a friend of mine was the Director. She called me and told me that I had to come and get Nicholas because he had bitten so many little children that morning. She said the parents might want to sue me. She thought there might be legal trouble. So I had to take him out of there and find a place for him. I found Sheltering Arms.

Nicholas had discipline problems in every grade. I had to go to the school so many times because of his discipline problems. His mother's cocaine addiction had a lot to do with it. Then at three years old he developed a kidney ailment; he retained fluid and bloated. He grew out of it, but it had an affect on him. He was one of the first children to be diagnosed with Attention Deficit Disorder, and they placed him on medication. Nicholas really didn't need it. I took him to every specialist you can name to find out if he had medical or mental problems. I think his problems were emotional, from when his mother left him. I remember when Nicholas was three and his mother was scheduled to pick him up and take him to a birthday party. She came to get him but had been out that night and was still under the influence. She came to the door and he ran to the door to see her. As she and I talked, Nicholas ran to get his coat. As he went to get his coat, she told me "I can't take him. I don't feel good today. I have a headache." She left before he came back. When that child came back to the door, he was devastated. I can see his face today. He was so sad. Tears came to my eyes. It hurt me so bad. I know it hurt him. From that day to this day, I believe that he has a grudge against his mother. He never mentioned her name. He never said that he wanted to stay with her. He never said that he wanted to go see her or anything. When he got older, at 13 or 14, he would ask about her. She made promises to him that when she got out of jail, she would go straight. But she never has. She has been in and out of jail for years. She gave custody of Nicholas to my brother and signed the papers when she was incarcerated.

What's your favorite story about each of your children?

My daughters and I would sit in the middle of the floor and have Bible study. Jennifer told me later on that they weren't listening. My children liked reading, but Jennifer didn't like to read as much as Jessica. Jessica loved to read. Even today, Jessica loves to read and write. She loves it. I never had to get on to them about doing their school work, although Jennifer did not like school that well.

For Jessica, school is fine, but she just wants to finish and get out. Jessica has always been an artist. When she was 6 or 7 years old, she drew an abstract of Martin Luther King. It looked just like him. She won many competitions the county held. I'll never forget when she wrote a poem, "Strawberry in a Glass." It was beautiful and won first place in the County. I remember her being passionate about her drawings and poems. She keeps journals of them too. She went to cosmetology school for two years and completed four years at Georgia Southern University, and didn't pursue that. She became a Massage Therapist. That's what she is doing now, but she wants to get her writings published one day.

Jessica did not learn to drive until she was out of school. She never had an interest in it. That's the kind of person she is. When she got her license, she drove to Atlanta, and she'd never driven before. It scared us to death. When she graduated from high school she waited a year to go to college because she wasn't ready. Her favorite job was cleaning the swimming pool at a motel in Austell. She liked it. She said she had a good job. Also, she took a job sitting in one of those Goodwill trailers, writing, and waiting for the people to bring their clothing. She liked that. Jennifer had a lot of fun laughing at her. But she didn't care that Jennifer laughed at her.

I enjoyed raising my daughters. I was really hard on them, though. If I had it to do all over, I think I would spend more time with them. The best part of raising them was being with them and dressing them; having fun with them. They didn't like to go shopping with my mother and me because we liked to shop. Jessica would hide under the clothing. Jennifer would have temper tantrums on the floor. That was before people would tell on you when you spanked your children. I spanked mine when they did something wrong.

We enjoyed having family gatherings. My husband was always working; he didn't see, at the time, the importance of quality time with our daughters. He was a City Councilman and he worked a lot at night, so my daughters spend a lot of time with me. My daughters were quite athletic. They played basketball in college and were quite good at it. But they didn't have a passion for it like Al and I did. They didn't like it well enough to make it a career.

What times did you most like spending with your children?

I loved to spend the holidays with my family; Fourth of July, Mothers' Day, Thanksgiving and Christmas. Easter was good too, but it was always difficult to find a dress that the girls liked.

Jennifer didn't like the normal things that I would pick. She liked the long earrings. If I had let her she would have put a ring in her nose and spiked hair. Jennifer was unique in her dressing style and Jessica didn't care much for clothes at all. Jennifer wears dreadlocks now. I'd fix Jennifer's hair and she didn't like it. She didn't want it pretty. She wanted it wild. That's why now she wears dreadlocks. Jessica was dainty and quiet. She would wear it, but clothing wasn't a big deal to her. They were as different as night and day.

Jennifer was just like her mother, in the sense that she was athletic. Whenever the guys needed a sixth person, they called on Jennifer. She could be friends with the guys. The girls didn't like her because she got along with the guys. I was like that. I had brothers. I knew how to do things that a lot of girls didn't know how to do.

My girls played sports. I used to love to see them play sports. I fixed their hair in afros and puffs. They played softball, basketball, ran track, took gymnastics, dance classes, and even piano. I tried to make them culturally sound. I exposed them to that as much as I could. They were good at what they did. Jennifer played the clarinet. Jessica played the saxophone. She liked that. After school, though, that was it. I tried to get them into a lot of activities so that they could pick and choose what they liked doing the most. Everybody's got to find themselves. I don't have any regrets because I exposed them, gave them alternatives, showed them what was out there, and they got to experience a lot of that. They knew how to make decisions.

What makes you proud of your children?

I'm proud of them because they're not ashamed of where they came from. My daughters would always accept what people gave them. They were never brand-name girls. They didn't look down on people. They tried to love everybody and be friends with everybody.

Jessica was like me, introverted in a lot of ways. She stayed by herself a lot, reading. I didn't like to be in the public. I didn't like being in the spotlight. I was always thrust into it. I enjoy talking to the Lord out loud. I enjoy reading. I do a lot of thinking and meditating.

My daughters see themselves in me. I see myself in both of my daughters. My oldest daughter, Jennifer is like me, a go-getter. She likes to have her own things, make her own way. Whatever she puts her mind to, she'll do it. You can depend on Jennifer to get the job done. Jessica is the part of me that is reserved and wants to be alone. She does her own thing at her own pace. I see myself in her. Jessica is quiet. She's always doing something. She stays in her room and reads and writes for hours. That's me. When I go home, I have my office. I have my cubby hole, and I can stay for hours and nobody will see or hear me. Sometimes I look up and see the wall and forget where I am. That's just me.

What would you like your children and grandchildren to remember about you?

That I love the Lord first, then I love people, and that I would help anybody that I could help. I want them to remember me as a hard worker. I love to work.

If you could write a message to each of your children and grandchildren and put it in a time capsule for them to read 20 years from now, what would you write to each?

I would tell each of them to establish their relationship with God. Get your Christian foundation and build on it.

Jennifer...I would tell her to go for it. Make sure your self esteem doesn't get low. Continue to know who you are and walk with your head up; not in a snooty way, but never look down. Always look up to Jesus. Work hard. Love people. Love yourself and you will be fine.

Jessica...that's my baby. I would tell her to establish her relationship with God. Hold onto it; never give up. She's a very persistent person, so I don't have to worry about her hanging in there. It's alright to spend some time alone, but never separate yourself totally from people because they have something that they can offer you and you would be surprised what you have to offer them. Love yourself. Don't ever look down or think anything bad about yourself. You are just as good as anybody else.

Nicholas (Nephew-Son)...establish your relationship with God. Work hard. Ask God to reveal to you who you are. There is so much inside of you that you don't even realize. I hope by now that you have found it because you are a very talented person, a very loving person, and you don't know how to use it. You've got a gold mine inside. You haven't tapped into it yet, so you need to discover that. Work hard and there's nothing that you can't do.

Lace (Granddaughter)...you're so pretty. You're smart, but you need to work harder. Begin to do the things that you love to do and you want to do. Stop sitting down. You have a personality to deal with people that surpasses those of your age. So get up from there and use your resources and your personality and go for it.

 Alex (Granddaughter)...so energetic. She has so much energy and she loves art. I hope you draw and will be able to share your paintings and your art with everybody, because that's your love. Don't ever leave it. You are so satisfied with it. You are so happy doing what you do. You are so innocent. Use that and stay with people. Love people. Keep that energy and make sure that it's in the right direction. Use it and continue to be Alex.

Langston (Grandson)...is a very smart and intelligent three year old. He can carry on a conversation. Continue to carry on that conversation. Be open. Be your own man. At three, I can see you are clawing at your own pace. He has a lot of initiative. He loves basketball. He loves any kind of ball; every sport he loves it—soccer, golf, volleyball, basketball, football, baseball. Pursue your dreams. Whatever he knows, he knows it. Whatever he's doing, he does it. Be persistent. Make sure that you establish your relationship with God first. Continue to develop what's inside you. Develop what you love to do. Be the best at it that you can be.

That's what I would tell all my children. Be the best at whatever it is you love to do. Strive to be the best; not compared with other people, but make sure you live up to your capacity. We want to get to the highest point in our lives that we can get. Reach the highest level that you can reach and be happy with it.

"Parenting a Child in the 21st Century: Building a Solid Foundation"
Women's Conference September 22, 2001

Like arrows in the hands of a warrior are sons born in one's youth. Blessed is the man whose quiver is full of them. They will not be put to shame when they contend with their enemies in the gate.

Psalm 127:4-5

God values families, calling children "a heritage from the Lord." Families are the foundation of society, the place where children are taught about faith in God and given love, nurture, and guidance. So why are there so many sad and separated families? Many families have ignored God in their family life, so He is not sought when the family faces troubles and difficulty. "Unless the Lord builds the house, they labor in vain who build it," wrote Solomon (Ps. 127:1). Putting the Lord at the base does not guarantee a perfect family; it does, however, provide a foundation upon which to build and guidelines by which to make decisions and handle difficulties. The family with God as its foundation will offer a solid, stable, and loving home. And it's never too late. This kind of foundation can always be laid, even under an existing house. The structure can then be remodeled on the firmest possible footing.

How many of you know that Godly parents have some of the worst children there is? You've seen that time and again, haven't you? We get more attention when children go wrong because there's an expectation that our children will be perfect. That's not the case; children often seem to exhibit their parent's faults more than their faith. It all started with Adam and Eve. The parents disobeyed God, and the children, at least one of the children, followed that example.

What does the Bible tell us about raising children? One thing we find about children in the Bible is that they were taught at an early age. I believe that to be one of the areas we fall short. What little bit we do, we do it too late. Instead of viewing everything our babies do as cute and responding "He's just a baby," we should teach right from wrong at the point where they do wrong.

"My people are fools; they do not know me. They are senseless children; they have no understanding. They are skilled in doing evil; they know not how to do good."
Jeremiah 4:22

How many agree with the way your parents raised you? (You don't have to raise your hand.) Because if you do, you are probably raising yours in most cases the same way. You can only teach what you know. Most of us got our information about child rearing by precepts, by knowledge and examples, and in some cases by trial and error. Parenting a child today is no different from the 1st century.

The problem was and still is that we didn't know how God wanted us to raise our children.

Our children are not mistakes. God wanted them here for a purpose. Our children are human beings; believe it or not, they have minds of their own, even if they don't seem to use them. We had nothing to do with a child being strong willed, or temperamental, or a passive child—they were born that way. Don't blame yourself.

Our children are confronted by drugs, alcohol, sex, and foul language wherever they turn, and of course the peer pressure on them is enormous. You're going to need the wisdom that can only come from God to deal with these situations.

You must accept the fact that your little angel is not perfect. Not all angels are perfect. *Even a child is known by his actions, by whether his conduct is pure and right.*

Prov. 20:11

Establish at an early age, even as babies, who the child is and who the parent is. Take charge of your children. Hold tightly to the reins of authority in the early days and build an attitude of respect during your brief window of opportunity. Once you have established your right to lead, begin to release, to give them a little leeway to test what they have been taught, as they mature.

Don't panic and give up the ship. Remember God didn't, and our parents didn't give up on us. Don't write them off, even when every impulse is to do just that. Our children need us now more than ever before.

Give them time to find themselves even if they appear not to be searching. Some children learn early who they are, while others may need to try out many different styles before they find their own personal expression. The important thing is to guide them into paths that are pleasing to God.

Most important, hold them up before the Lord in fervent prayer throughout their years. God and His word is the greatest source of confidence and wisdom in parenting our children. Knowing God builds confidence and knowing God builds courage. Bathe them in prayer every day of their lives. The God who made our children will hear our petitions. He has promised to do so. After all, He loves them more than we do. Remember, anyone can raise a good easy child. But raising a rebellious, strong-willed child takes a pro. The devil wants our children. So it's going to be a fight. The next time your child wants to talk back or be rebellious in other ways, start to put on your armor and pray!

Study and Reflection

Hear, O Israel: The Lord our God, the Lord is one. Love the Lord your God with all your heart and with all your soul and with all your strength. These commandments that I give you today are to be upon your hearts. Impress them on your children. Talk about them when you sit at home and when you walk along the road, when you lie down and when you get up.   Deuteronomy 6:4-7

What do we learn from these verses?

What does God tell us about raising our children?

What is the first and most important instruction that children should receive, according to the Bible?

How should we instruct our children in the ways of the Lord?

CHAPTER NINE
The Church

And let us consider one another to provoke unto love and to good works: Not forsaking the assembling of ourselves together, as the manner of some is; but exhorting one another: and so much the more, as ye see the day approaching.

Hebrews 10:24,25

Earlier, you talked about going to church as a child and some of the activities that you remember. What else do you remember about going to church when you were young?

At the early age of thirteen I remember going to a revival. My cousins lived over the road from us, two or three miles away and they would come and join us. That particular night we had a ride, but most of the nights we had to walk. We had to begin walking early in order to make it in time for service. We would start walking around 5:00 pm in order to make it to the 7:30 pm service. On the way back we would ask somebody to give us a ride back home. This one time it was really hot in church and the church was full. My cousins, all of us went to church that night. We sat on the front pew. I remember the pianist and the choir. I remember the psalmist singing. That particular service is very clear in my mind.

I remember going to Vacation Bible School, as well. I remember some of the Bible stories. I remember one night when there was a big storm. I didn't even know how to pray but I remember getting down on my knees saying "Lord, I just want to go to heaven with you." From that time on, there was something special about church. I loved going to church.

How are you involved with your church today?

The work I do for church is my life. I'm serious. I love church. I love to see people happy and rejoicing in the Lord. We were never really taught the Bible, but we had a big Bible that sat on our coffee table in the living room that you didn't touch. You couldn't touch the Bible when I was coming up. In church when I was young, they never read anything but a scripture before they preached and everybody was going to heaven or hell, fire and brimstone. They taught the Lord's Prayer and the 23rd Psalm. That's the only thing that I remember.

Another thing about church that I loved; my mother and eight sisters, practically all of them shouted. I mean they shouted. It was something about the shouting. My mother would shout and she would cry. They wore hats and their hats would come off. They'd swing their pocketbooks and the wooden benches would rock. You'd have to get up because the ushers would come and hold them. It would be hot. The preacher would take off his coat because he was sweating. The children would stand in the corner just looking. We were looking; it was exciting to us. I always watched my mother. I knew what she had been going through during the week because I was right there with her. When they finished shouting, their burdens were gone. They walked out of church and they were happy. We'd go home and play church. We had a great time imitating those people at the church.

"Unity of the Spirit"

May 18th 2003
Faith Missionary Baptist Church

To look at you all, one might think you were all together, and one could be right in thinking that. You know, before I got married almost 35 years ago, my husband would always say, "Yes, you're right honey." I was always right. Then after I got married, I started being wrong all the time. My mother once told me, "Baby, you don't have to know everything, just be able to ask somebody who knows everything. So now, if I have a question I just ask my husband, he knows everything. [laughter]

I know your emphasis this afternoon is on women, but God gave me "Unity of the Spirit" as my topic. In Ephesians 4:3, Paul tells us to "make every effort to keep the Unity of the Spirit through the bond of peace." Before you can stay in or keep the unity, you must first have unity. Where do you get unity? From the Holy Spirit. How do you get the Holy Spirit? You don't, you must be born again. God is the perfect Unity—Father, Son, and Holy Spirit. To get the Holy Spirit, you must first have God in your heart.

To be in unity in the body, you must have love, agreement, and togetherness. The first requirement is love. Scripture says in Matthew 22:37 to love with your heart and soul and mind; Mark adds strength. Now, if you don't love the Lord, we need to stop right there, because you can't be in unity without loving God. Do you all love God with your whole heart and mind and soul and strength?

The second commandment is to love your neighbor as yourself. You must love yourself before you can love your neighbor. Do you think anyone in here looks better than you? If so you have a self-esteem problem, you don't love yourself. The Bible says in Psalm 139 that we are wonderfully made. Do you know who you are in Christ? You are accepted – secure – significant – a valuable piece of dirt. There are no stars in Christ's Church. Stars fall – we are servants. Christ is the only one in His Church who makes a difference. He works through us.

To be in unity, you must be in agreement. In the Bible, agreement means a covenant, a sacred contract between God and you. In order to agree, we have to know and believe the same things. Paul says in 1 Corinthians 1:10 "I appeal to you brethren, by the name of our Lord Jesus Christ, that ye all speak (agree) the same thing, and that there be no discussions among you but that ye be perfectly joined (united) together in the same mind and thought (judgment)." The Bible is what we must know and believe.

Everything we do and say should be based on the rightly divided Word of God.

There's a difference between God works and Godly works. The "O" in good stands for obedience to God's direction through His word. "Not my will but Thy will be done." You may do a lot of good things, but only what you do for Christ will last. In Matthew 7:21-23, Jesus says that works alone without God's direction are fruitless.

So be very careful; what you do for Christ is not nearly as important as what you do with Christ. Whatever you do, if He didn't lead you to do it, it's going to be burnt up as stubble.

There's no room for competition and jealousy. You know what jealousy is? Pastor Charles Stanley refers to it in one of his devotional books as nothing more than you having a conflict with God over what He's doing in another person's life.

To be in unity, you must have togetherness. I do not see why we can't work together if we are following God's direction. God has the master plan, and we are just working on a little piece of the plan, like the children of Israel rebuilding the temple. Each group had a specific job, but together they created God's temple according to God's blueprint.

If you are going to dwell together in unity, you are going to have to forget about pleasing woman or man. Woman is not pleased with herself most of the time anyway; she needs more hair, more holes for jewelry, etc...so you know you can't please her. God didn't please Adam and Eve; God didn't please the Children of Israel; Noah preached for 120 years and people didn't pay him any attention. The same is true today; nothing has changed.

My last point is – Don't gossip. Gossip separates that person who gossips and only reveals the evil in their own hearts. Matthew 12:33-34 says, "Make a tree good and its fruit will be good." Tune those gossipers out. They're not going to do anything useful. Separate yourself. You'll never be together listening to Sister So-and-So if she talks about anybody other than Jesus. Gossip destroys your fellowship with God. It really doesn't matter what others say, it's what God says. In my line of work...you can believe I don't have time to gossip, I'm too busy trying to get the spots and wrinkles out of my life.

If God can love me and put up with me even when I didn't know and believe in Him, surely I can love you in spite of your faults, seeing how I have so many of my own.

CHAPTER TEN
Faith

Then Jesus answered, "Woman, you have great faith! Your request is granted."

Matthew 15:28

You are known as a woman of strong faith and conviction. Tell me about your strength and how you got to this point.

I know who I am in Christ. I don't need anyone to tell me who I am. I don't need anybody's approval to know who I am. That's the most important thing, because I can be anything in Christ. If I allow him to, he will make me be the best I can be. When I reach that particular point I'm satisfied. It may not be as good as yours, but it's the best that I can do. I'm content with it. Praise the Lord.

When I was a child, I feared God's thunder. I feared people getting in trouble. I feared death. It hurt me to hear that somebody died, or that they were hurt or killed. Now, when I hear of people dying, it hurts my heart, but I am not alarmed or fearful of it. It makes me cry. When tornados come, I pray, because I know that it's in the hands of the Lord; whereas back then, I didn't know much about things being in the hands of the Lord.

Earlier in my life, I would tithe first, and then I would give offerings. Now I would give the bulk of it to the church. I know that you can't beat God in giving. It is more blessed to give than to receive.

If you could have three wishes, what would they be?

My first wish would be to be financially able to put money into the ministry at my church. My second wish would be for all of my relatives to be saved. I want them to know the joy of the Lord. My third wish would be to have my own academy and school so that I could teach and train students, and hire people that have the like vision that I have.

"Who's on Watch?"

Deliverance Baptist Church
October 1, 2006

Good afternoon, greetings to you.

You are celebrating your usher's anniversary. That's wonderful. You all had to agree on something's because I haven't seen you in the court house filing law suits against each other. I haven't issued any warrants for your arrest for shooting at one another, beating up on one another. And that's a good thing. The Bible tells us plainly what to do with one another's burdens, comfort one another and tell one another the truth and on and on.

Don't fool yourself, just because you go to church or call yourself a Christian doesn't mean you are not guilty of these criminal offenses. In my almost twenty years, I have ordered the arrest of pastors, preachers, evangelists, choir members, deacons, ushers and the like. Let me leave that alone; some of you will be calling me trying to find out who they are. [laughter]

I say this everywhere I go; as I get over into the afternoon of my life, the Lord is making me more and more aware of the importance of maximizing each moment, more aware of my purpose, more aware of what I do with the 24 hours He has given me each day. For I realize that I will have to give account for every thought, every word, and every deed done in this body. The Bible says in Romans 14:12, "For every one of us must give account to God for himself." I'm not that concerned with what others may say about me because I know that God has not placed any of us here on earth in charge of heaven or hell. So I'm concerned more about what the Lord Jesus says about me. How about you?

Let's talk about who's on watch. That's interesting because nosy folks no doubt will ask—watching for what? Or who? There's always someone watching. Watching to see where you are going, to see who you are with, to see what you're wearing, to see what kind of car you are driving, how long you hold the pastor's hand, who the pastor's wife smiles at, who's in the pastor's office, all of which means absolutely nothing. That's not important, that's not going to change anybody's sinful heart. There are more serious issues we need to be addressing.

The Bible tells us in I Thessalonians 5:6, "Therefore let us not sleep, as do others; but let us watch and be sober." My understanding of what the apostle Paul is saying is simply that as believers we have been delivered from darkness of sin and ignorance. Because we are children in the light we should not sleep in spiritual indifference and our comfort, but be alert to the spiritual issues around us. Some of the things we ought to be watching include our homes and families, some of which are being destroyed by drugs. Our sons and daughters are so strung out on drugs they are becoming thieves and robbers to support their $1500 to $2000 habits. Our daughters are becoming prostitutes even on the internet, selling their bodies to support their habits, getting pregnant and then leaving their babies in trash cans, trash bags, on door steps. Some are even aborting their babies because some states have laws that say they have a right to do so.

We need to watch how our children are using foul, vulgar and obscene language, how they dress, like gang members, thugs, hoochie mamas, tattooed and pierced in places where the sun should never shine or the moon should never glow. You know what I'm talking about.

We need to watch how our young people are filling up the jail houses; and even if they do get out, they can't function. They have gotten caught up in the system. They are being killed accidentally and on purpose; whether accidentally or on purpose, they are still dead. Our children are becoming open air gays and lesbians with no shame, HIV positive, which is rising especially in our culture. They are out of control and sinking further every day.

We need to be watching our husband and wives who are leaving each other and giving up on marriage at an alarming rate. People are deciding to just live together; when they get tired of that so-call partner, they move on to the next one. Half of the people who get married are getting a divorce. We should be watching how we live in front of our children at home and in the church house. They are only going to respect what they see and hear and, as my mama use to say, and feel.

We need to be watching at the church house. No longer is it enough just for the pastor to watch over our souls, you'd better be watching for your own behind. And you can't just be watching for your own behind; you can't just be an usher standing at the door frowning—oh, I mean smiling—handing out programs, fans, and envelopes. You have to be mindful of every person, someone who is caught up in evil could come to church shooting and killing anyone in sight. They aren't concerned about the Father, the Son or the Holy Ghost. We have to be aware of those incidents and be on watch.

I Peter 4:7 say, "But the end of all things is at hand; be ye therefore sober and watch unto prayer." The time is near when all things will end. So think clearly and control yourselves, so you will be able to pray.

My brothers and sisters, we need to watch. Christ has given to us the ministry of reconciliation. We all have the responsibility to do something about the horrible conditions we find ourselves in. Getting the Word out to the people so they will know the truth is up to us, not just pastors, preachers, and teachers. We must be who we say we are all the time.

In God's eyes—who sees everything, and knows everything, and is everywhere at the same time—there are no special people or special positions. We all are here to share the good news. Have you told anyone today, yesterday, last week?

Who's on watch….we all are or we'd better be. For we must remember, there's always somebody watching and His name is Jesus. And I'm glad about that. I ain't about to give up. I don't care how bad it looks; I know God is still in charge.

CHAPTER ELEVEN
Holidays

Every good and perfect gift is from above, coming down from the Father of the heavenly lights, who does not change like shifting shadows.

James 1:17 (NIV)

What was your favorite holiday as a child?

Christmas was my favorite holiday because that's what we called Jesus' birthday. That time of the year was special because of Jesus Christ and the love that he shared with me, from a child up. Christmas holiday taught me how to be thankful. It taught me how to love and cherish little things, like getting oranges and apples, because we didn't get those through the year. We got them at Christmastime, and a few nuts and peppermint candy. My mother would put them in a shoebox. On Christmas, you went and found your shoebox. It made the whole house smell like Christmas. We had to go out to the woods and get our Christmas tree. It was just special. At that time, they didn't have black pictures of Jesus; only white ones. It was just Jesus, thankfully. I can appreciate whatever I get.

In school, we celebrated every holiday. My favorite holiday was Christmas because we got to draw on the windows. We got to paint the Santa Claus, the sleighs and reindeers, snowflakes, Christmas trees on the windows. I used to love it. They would give us a copy of some Christmas scene that you could color. I used to love that. We would bring them home and momma would hang them up on the wall. When it snowed, they would let us go to the window and see the snowflakes fall. It was just beautiful, calm and peaceful.

I don't remember much about the bad things that happened during that time because I was just so happy with life. I loved life.

Can you remember any gift that you received as a child that was the best gift?

It was a camera. My mother gave it to me for Christmas. My mother's sister gave her daughter one too. It was a camera you snapped from your waist. It was called a 'snapshot.' We very seldom bought film for the camera because we didn't have any money. My mother bought me one because my cousin had one and she wanted me to have one. I remember having dolls but dolls were not really my thing. My mom tried to get me a doll every year but I wasn't really into dolls.

How did your family celebrate Thanksgiving?

Momma cooked. We didn't have turkeys. We had hens. She would cook, cook, cook, and we would eat, eat, and eat. It was special, but we had big meals almost all the time. My mother had to cook a lot because I had four brothers that ate a lot. The only difference is that she would bake cakes and pies during the holidays. We had a lot of Thanksgiving holidays.

Do you have special memories of other holidays?

Oh, Easter was great. My mother would try her best to get us special outfits for Easter. It was just great! I have the picture now of the dress I wore one Easter. My mother would sprinkle our clothes with starch and iron them. She didn't go to the store to buy starch; she made it. By that time, we had an electric iron. Before that, we had the iron that you had to put on top of the stove and let it get hot.

I remember going to church on what we called, "May Day Singing." The food was just great. We had fried chicken and sweet potato custard. Every family would bring a box of food. They had this big table and had all kinds of food and desserts on it. You'd go around the table and get what you wanted. We had service in the morning. Everyone had on their pretty hats. We had on our Easter outfits, very colorful. The church was so full you couldn't get in. It was the best time. A photographer would come and take pictures. Sometimes we got our picture taken. We usually didn't have the money. One time my brother and I took a picture together. Today, I have it somewhere at the house. They would have snow cones. A snow cone was good, if you got one. It was a relief at the end of the day when we walked back home on that hot pavement. We were tired, but happy. We had a great time.

Is the present better or worse than when you were younger?

It is better. Every day with Jesus is sweeter than the day before. That's a song. [Singing] That's very true. I mean, I have my human moments. When the devil starts throwing things at me, and he started throwing things at me yesterday, I say "Devil you are a liar." I realize that the devil tries to upset me. It's getting easier to put the problems and concerns in the hands of the Lord and try to focus on what he would have me to do. The Bible tells us to cast our cares upon him and I seek Him first and all the other things are added to me. I am trying my best to do what the Lord says do. If I do that, it's going to be better for me. He's going to take care of me if I allow him, in every area.

"Facing the Storm"

The Bible is the most important book in the World. It has withstood the test of time. It is still new; it will never get old. I can appreciate Oprah's efforts in trying to get people to read more, but for the Christian . . . it would benefit us greatly to see what this book – the BIBLE – has to say about living in today's society.

Let's look at the natural storm clouds that often appear well before a storm. When we see storm clouds, we take action; we find a place to take cover, we close the windows and doors, we find our umbrellas. For the Christian, the storm clouds are appearing. We should take action to prepare for the coming storm. We need to spend time in prayer, to scan the horizon of the day for telltale signs of difficulty. When we sense a storm is developing, we can find sanctuary, a refuge from the storm. I am sensing a coming storm. We are living in a time when society observes gay pride festivals, condones adultery, and labels violence as entertainment. We say, "It's just something to do, another part of life, no big deal." But every day, we see reports of domestic violence, fighting in courtrooms and TV stations and ball fields, murder in schools, cloning, and the list goes on and on.

What is the cure? What is the answer? What is the solution? The same as it's always been! Jesus Christ. I want to talk to you about focus, staying focused. In Romans 12: 1 and 2, Paul says to live in this world; a child of God must be separated, educated, and insulated.

In order to stay focused, we must first be separated. The Word says, "Come from among them and be ye separated." We must make a clear distinction between clean and unclean. Jesus separates us from the world. Jesus has to do the separating, because we are all worldly. We pay attention to worldly instructions – stop smoking, eat more vegetables, wear seat belts, stay out of the sun, lose weight, volunteer. All good and fine, but we need to focus on God the Father, God the Son, and God the Holy Spirit. What does He say?

The first and greatest commandment is *"Thou shall love the Lord . . . ." "God so loved the world . . . ." "to know God is to have eternal life . . . ." "sin has separated us from God. . . ." "No man can come to the Father except . . . ." "Jesus said, I stand at the door . . . ." "But to as many as receive Him . . . ." "If any man comes unto Me, I will . . . ." "just as Moses lifted up the serpent . . . ."* So if He's all that – and He is – what's the problem? Why are you not saved? To be separated, you must be born again.

In order to stay focused, we must also be educated. Paul told Timothy to study. The Bible is full of exhortations to gain knowledge. "You can't do more than you know . . . . You can't be ignorant of Satan's devices . . . . Ye shall know the truth and the truth . . . . Jesus is truth . . . . These things are written . . . . Knowledge is the beginning of . . . . truth and error – Jesus said, Take My yoke upon you and learn . . . .Search the scripture. In the book of Hosea, God says *"My people are destroyed through lack of knowledge."* In Jeremiah, God says, *"I will give you pastors and teachers."* Peter says, *"Be ready to give an answer for the hope that is in you."* The Word is God's expression of himself, a declaration of His will and works.

To stay focused, we must also be insulated. Ephesians 6:13 says *"Take unto you the whole armor of God."* If you are wearing armor, you can withstand persecution, ridicule, challenges, and even attacks.

The storm clouds are gathering. The Bible tells us how to get ready for the storm and how to withstand the storm, but what about after the storm?

After the storm, it will be known whose house was built on the rock—the Word, on Jesus—and whose house was built on sand—religious works, good deeds, empty words. Do not use your life as a bridge to build on, use your life as a bridge to cross over on. We are not here to stay, so don't unpack. The only thing Jesus is coming back for is His church. Stay focused. Be not conformed to this world, but be ye transformed by the renewing of your mind.

Whatsoever you do, do all to the glory of God.

CHAPTER TWELVE
Black History

There is neither Jew nor Greek, there is neither bond nor free, there is neither male nor female: for ye are all one in Christ Jesus.

Galatians 3:28 (NIV)

When did you first become aware of the separation between the black community and the white? How did that impact your life?

I remember our first television. Our first television was black and white. We would put clear colorful plastic over the television. That would be our color television. If we saw a black man on TV as a butler; it didn't matter what he was, we would run and yell "Momma! There's a black man on TV!" All of us would run to the TV, sit and watch him. We thought it was something to see black people on television. We were so proud to see them on TV; Amos and Andy. We were so proud of that show. We loved to see those kinds of shows and any show that you saw a black person.

We didn't know much about racism. My mother never taught that. I knew there was a difference, but I never questioned it, for some reason. I was content with what I was doing, with what I had. When we went to pick beans, we'd get on the back of the truck. White people would sit on the front and we'd sit on the back but it didn't bother me. I didn't feel inferior. It was my job so I went and did it. For a whole week we made $25 picking beans. Our goal was to have a telephone, so the whole family went out to the field and worked. My mother still has the same telephone number she first got back then.

Do you have any concerns for the future?

I don't see black people advancing and that bothers me. That is a great concern of mine. I totally agree with Bill Cosby. If we would spend time teaching our children how to live rather than make a living, learning how to be parents to our children, we would be better off. We are so materialistic until we forget about quality of life, and that is killing us. I'm concerned about that.

I'm concerned about the plight and the course that my country is in. But there is nothing that I can do about that, other than vote for the right person that I think is God-conscious, and contact my Congressman or Congresswoman. Besides that, I pray.

I believe that I am responsible for the things that I can do within my own race, because I am black. Then I'm responsible for people, because I am a person. I'm responsible for parents because I am a parent. And I am serious about these responsibilities.

"Growing in His Grace"

Therefore, dear friends, since you already know this, be on your guard so that you may not be carried away by the error of lawless men and fall from your secure position. But grow in the grace and knowledge of our Lord and Savior Jesus Christ. To Him be glory both now and forever! Amen

We—Black people, people of color, African Americans, did I miss anybody?—We are in trouble. We may have been delivered and freed from slavery, but we are still slaves.

We are slaves to what we allow to control us—including our thoughts, our conduct, the clothes we wear, how we raise our children, even how we fix our hair. We are slaves to violence, to drugs, to gangs, to the probation officer and yes, even to each other, how we treat one another.

You may say "What does this have to do with me?" Well...look at "Growing in His Grace." Growing implies progress, getting better and maturing. And how much progress as a people have we made? Martin Luther King said, "The door of opportunity has opened; will we seize it, take advantage of it, and go in before it begins to close again?"

We are not prepared to complete this growing. It is our responsibility, yours and mine, to help prepare our young people to complete what has been started. Young people, my heart goes out to you. God is using this Organization to equip you for the next level of preparation for his return. Look ahead with confidence not in ourselves but in God and in the power of His might (Eph 6:10). Jesus has saved us for the purpose of reflecting His life in our work, our ways, and our words. Our lives should be an expression of God's grace.

There are going to be people out there who won't trust you. Why; because of your skin color. That's all right; there will be some people out there that you don't trust, maybe because of their skin color. But I hope you will remember what God said; "Put not your trust in man."

It has been said that we are fools. The basic difference between the wise man/woman and the fool is in the use each makes of his time, talent, and material possessions. It has been said that we buy what we want and beg for what we need. Those of us who have God-given blessings cannot be indifferent or self-satisfied. Such an abundance of divine grace calls for total dedication. That dedication means making a maximum effort to help others come into the knowledge of the truth. Isn't that what the other part of the verse means? We are to be wary of false knowledge and avoid those who don't follow the teachings of Christ.

God said in Hosea 4:6, "My people are destroyed for lack of knowledge."

Do you seek to be righteous followers of Christ? Get your heart right toward God. Do you earnestly seek God's will for your life? And do you trust God's promises? If so, then you will be faithful stewards of the gifts and talents He has given you.

Oswald Chambers advised, "Never support an experience which does not have God as its source, and faith in God as its result." And so it is with our lives, our positions, the organizations we may be a member of—when we return our lives back to God, we will experience the spiritual growing in His Grace that always accompanies obedience to Him. Only then will we develop that love, understanding and likeness of Christ.

I hope that our focus on Black history is not and will not be limited to any one month, or year, or even decade. Assuredly, great contributions and sacrifices for mankind were made throughout the years in times past. First, I will give honor to God, for without Him we would not be celebrating anybody's history.

CHAPTER THIRTEEN
Helping People

In Joppa there was a disciple named Tabitha (which, when translated, is Dorcas), who was always doing good and helping the poor.

Acts 9:36

What do you enjoy best about your job?

Back in 1986, I had been a Magistrate part-time and they were looking for someone full time. At that time, they had about 4 or 5 part-timers. One Tuesday night, the Chief Magistrate, Steve Messenger, called me at home and asked me if I would take the position because they thought I was the one that would better serve, and my reason for serving was different from other people. Steven interviewed me. He said that he liked the reason that I wanted to be Magistrate. It was a low paying job. I came into the job making less than $20,000 per year, full time. It wasn't the money. I liked the fact that I could help people.

The best compliment I've ever received was "you helped me." When somebody says to me, "You helped me," it's the greatest reward I could get.

Back in the 1980s, I worked for the Internal Revenue Service part time. I passed the test and became a Taxpayer Representative. I enjoyed talking to people on the phone. At the time, you were being monitored by your supervisors. Sometimes, I'd forget that the calls were possibly being monitored. We had a lot of irate tax payers. Sometimes I would be talking to an irate customer; by the time we hung up the phone we were just talking about different things like their children, their dogs. I would do my job. One day my supervisors called me to the back and I thought I was in trouble. There were people back there that I didn't know. They presented me with an award and a reward of $300. They recognized my people skills and my ability to handle tax payers. That was a special moment in my life. I didn't realize that they were listening and that it meant anything. To this day, I have the letter. It was awesome to me. I received other awards but they don't mean as much as that one did. It just goes to show that you can have an influence on other people no matter where you are, as long as you have the right spirit in your heart.

"Has the Church Lost Its Savor?"

St. James AME Church
125TH Church Anniversary
July 15, 2007

Shout for joy to the Lord, all the earth. Worship the Lord with gladness; come before him with joyful songs. Know that the Lord is God. It is He, who made us, and we are his; we are his people, the sheep of his pasture. Enter his gates with thanksgiving and his courts with praise; give thanks to him and praise his name. For the Lord is good and his love endures forever; his faithfulness continues through all generations.
Psalm 100:1-5

It is an honor to be asked to come and share in this great celebration of 125 years of this body in the church of the Lord Jesus Christ.

In Matthew 16:18, our Lord speaks, "And I say also unto thee, that thou are Peter and upon this rock I will build my church, and the gates of Hell shall not prevail against it."

And in the 5th chapter, verse 13, He says, "Ye are the salt of the earth; but if the salt hath lost its savor, wherewith shall it be salted? It is thenceforth good for nothing but to be cast out and to be trodden under the foot of men."

My question this morning is "Has the church lost its savor?"

As you know, the African Methodist Episcopal Church was founded by Richard Allen who was born a slave in Philadelphia, Pennsylvania, to the family of Benjamin Chew. He was later sold to a planter in Dover, Delaware, where he grew to manhood. There he came under Christian influence and was converted in 1777. A few years later, he began to preach. His master was so impressed by his genuineness, he allowed Allen to conduct prayer meetings and preach in his house. He himself was one of the first to be converted by this zealous messenger of God.

Reverend Allen was driven by a great desire to meet the needs of Black people who had long been overlooked and were a forgotten people when it came to Christian education. He was aware of the scripture Hosea 4:6 where God says "My people are destroyed for they lack knowledge."

You see back in his days, the days of slavery long before the missionaries deliberately preached Christianity to the slaves, the slaves had found a close companionship with God on their own cultural terms and in their own way. Prayers were born in the fields, where the slaves spent most of their lives. They were primarily prayers for freedom and deliverance and for their children to see a better day.

This companionship and intimacy Black people found in prayer is reflected historically in their having some special place for prayer. They called it the "Praise House," a building where the slaves would gather nightly for the purpose of praying, singing, dancing, and praising God.

Pastor Andrew Bryan was another one of the first noted among Black people who founded his church with prayer meetings. These prayer meetings planted the seed for an all-important movement, the church.

Out of the traditional prayer meeting evolved a full-blown worship service. So much so that Pastor Bryan and his brother became targets for persecution. They were often spied on, and the eavesdroppers would report to the authorities what was going on in the Praise House. In the meantime, Pastor Bryan, his brother, and the others who were gathered in this new church prayed not themselves but for the men who so unmercifully used and persecuted them.

As a result of their prayers, they found favor and sympathy among the people in authority. So when they were brought before the Chief Justice of the court, they were granted permission to continue their worship of God anytime between sunrise and sunset. Talk about the savor of prayer! You remember the old song "Let Jesus Fix It, For He Knows Just What to Do."

What I'm trying to say is "what has happened to our prayer savor? The Black Church that started out as a prayer meeting is the very foundation of our freedom. Satan, the god of this world, has blinded minds and ears. Our freedom is slowly being taken away. We have been drawn away from the main thing by our many ministries designed to get everyone involved. It seems like we are attempting to please the people. "I'm not going to church today, we aren't singing," "That church is boring, ain't nothing to do." We are doing more socializing than fellowshipping. We have replaced "sho' nuff genuine" prayer service with prayer visuals. Praise teams are okay, but you can't substitute one for the other. Whatever happened to praying until your spirit is broken, praying until we received an answer from God? People would weep and mourn with tears of "Thank You Lord," and tears of "I need you Lord; I can't make it by myself." The old hymns, "Precious Lord, Take My Hand," "What a Friend We Have in Jesus," "Real, Real Jesus is Real to Me," "I Come to the Garden Alone," "Father, I Stretch My

Hand to Thee," "Blessed Assurance," "Jesus, Keep Me Near the Cross."

If you have to entertain people with these rock songs, movies, plays and programs to get them in church, they don't need to be there. They need to be in a night club or a bar and grill, a football stadium, a basketball arena. Jesus said, "If I be lifted up from the earth, I will draw all men unto me." We don't need to be entertained when our children are being deprived of their fathers and mothers by unlawful acts of authority figures and by each other. Our young people are arming themselves with weapons and guns, not to protect themselves from the law, but from each other. The majority of our young people who have been killed are killed by other people of color.

There's nothing new under the sun. There's nothing new about the death of an unarmed father being shot while he lay on the ground by a white deputy sheriff in Columbus, Georgia. There's nothing new about the lynching of Bernard Burden, a young Black man found hanged in the yard of his white girlfriend in Grantsville, Georgia. There's nothing new about the senseless shooting death of an unarmed, 22-year-old Black man by a white police officer in Commerce, Georgia. These are just a few known cases since 2003. Scripture says, "Many are the afflictions of the righteous, but the Lord delivereth him out of them all."

There's nothing new about the Genarlow Wilson case. There are many harsh, unfair, cruel and unjust laws still on the books, but for just a time as this, I believe God will expose and uncover some of the atrocities that are happening to people, not just Black people.

We need to answer the question Moses asked the children of Israel, "Who's on the Lord's side?" We need to take back the responsibility of raising our children. When I was coming up, you couldn't wear just any old thing to church. Young women are dressing as if they are asking to be abused and misused. Our young people are dating at 10, 11, and 12 years old, going to parties and proms after graduating from elementary and middle schools. Our 3 and 4 year olds are using curse words that sailors used. Parents allow their children to talk back. Children and young people are striking and killing their parents and grandparents. Our children are bringing weapons to school to inflict harm upon their classmates. I'm talking about elementary school. Parents are starving their children to death, drowning them in bathtubs and lakes, hanging them in closets, leaving them with boyfriends, giving them overdoses of drugs, exposing them to all kinds of sexual acts.

All of this is going on and the church is standing this Sunday teaching you how to get a car from God, how to get a house from God, believing God for a husband. You need to talk to someone who has one and see if you really want one! [laughter] We are teaching prosperity to get people to come to church, using Mark 11:24. God is not talking about things you can see, feel, or touch.

Every time we come to church, we hear about choir anniversaries, while a son is in jail. We hear about an upcoming play, while a husband is not acting right. We hear about the missionary society's tea on Saturday, while many don't know how to get rid of the stress in their minds and get some peace in their minds. Our churches are preaching about how to get more stuff; I don't need any more stuff. I want you to tell me how to walk in peace; I want you to tell me how to walk in love.

I don't come to church to find out how to get a car; I can get one of them financed. I don't come to church to find out how to get a house. I can get one of them financed. What I want to know is who's gonna finance the misery in my soul; I want to hear a word from the Lord. I want something money can't buy, police can't kill, and the jails can't hold. If you ask God for something and you believe the answer is in His Word, you shall have what you ask. The Word of God changes lives. God said in his Word, "If my people who are called by my name shall humble themselves, and pray, and seek My face, and turn from their wicked ways, then will I hear from heaven, and will forgive their sins, and will heal their land."

There's an old saying "You can lead a horse to water but you can't make him drink." But I say if you give him enough salt, he'll drink. Has the church lost its savor?

Study and Reflection

The greatest competition of true devotion to Jesus is the service we do for Him. Am I more devoted to service than I am to Jesus Christ Himself? How does my time reflect my commitment?

How many hours do I spend every week with God—in prayer, just talking to God and listening to Him, and reading and studying the Bible?

How many hours do I spend every week attending church services?

How many hours do I spend every week doing the work of the Church – making calls, preparing meals, attending meetings, writing letters, etc?

What does my time reflect about my relationship with God?

How can I rearrange my time and my commitments so that I can spend more time with God?

We don't consciously and deliberately disobey God. We simply don't listen to Him. God has given His commands, but we pay no attention to them, not because of willful disobedience but because we simply do not love and respect Him.

Am I aware of God's presence in my life every day?

Do I take the time to stop and just listen to God in my prayer time?

Am I aware of God's will for my life every time I make a decision?

It is not that I don't want to hear God, but I am not devoted in the right areas of my life. I am devoted to things and given to service. The attitude of a child of God should always be, "Speak, Lord, for your servant hears."

CHAPTER FOURTEEN
Aging

And even to your old age I am he; and even to hoar hairs will I carry you: I have made, and I will bear; even I will carry, and will deliver you.

Isaiah 46:4 (NIV)

How do you feel about growing old?

My feeling about aging is this. Life is morning, afternoon and evening. I am now in the afternoon of my life. The sun is shining bright and everything is fine. When I get older I'll be in the evening time of my life. That's the way I feel.

Do you have any expectations about what growing older would be like?

I expect me to be doing what I'm doing until the Lord calls me home. I expect him to give me strength, the stamina, everything that I need to do his Will. That's why I try to eat right, exercise, get physical exams, do everything that I need to do to keep myself physically fit. My outlook on life is to make sure that I do what I can do to prevent problems. I am a preventive person. If I feel a cold coming, I take something. I don't wait until I get the cold.

If I feel a headache coming, I do something about it. I'm looking to have the strength to continue. I may not be going as fast as I'm going now, but I'll be going. When I'm older I may not think as quickly and clearly as I do now but I expect to be thinking. I believe the Lord will help me.

My advice is to do what you can do for yourself, to keep yourself going. You know that you have to have food; eat the right foods. Drink water if you need it. You know that it's not good to smoke, don't smoke. Don't do things to hurt yourself. Sin and the world are going to be working against you anyway. Don't work against yourself. Be happy. Enjoy life. Laugh. Don't get too serious. Longevity in life is in Christ Jesus. He wants us to have life more abundantly. Eternal life has already begun with me.

Is the present better or worse than when you were younger?

It is better. Every day with Jesus is sweeter than the day before. That's a song. [Singing] That's very true. I mean, I have my human moments. When the devil starts throwing things at me, and he started throwing things at me yesterday. I say, "Devil, you are a liar." I realize that the devil tries to upset me. It's getting easier to put the problems and concerns in the hands of the Lord and try to focus on what he would have me to do. The Bible tells us to cast our cares upon him, and if I seek Him first then all the other things are added to me. I am trying my best to do what the Lord says do. If I do that, it's going to be better for me. He's going to take care of me if I allow him, in every area.

What have you thrown away in your life that you wish you hadn't?

Time....time....time. I wish I had applied myself and used my time more wisely than I have. I remember a lot of things I could have done. I remember times in my earlier years of dating and marriage when I was trying to find things to do, but now it's not enough time to do what I want to do. I can sit and read a book, study the Word of God, get prepared for my class for hours, but then I have to stop because I know I have to get some rest. But when I get up, I'm ready to go. I have an urgency about me now that I did not use to have...a passion for children to learn, to get educated because they are going to need it. The competition is getting stiff and I'm mighty afraid that our young people will be left behind.

What have you held onto that is important and why is it important?

My love for God, My love for the Church, and My love for his work. It's important. If I don't hold on to that, then I'm not going to be anything. He's the foundation of my life. Without Him I couldn't make it. I know that I couldn't. I've held on to my relationship with the Lord. I keep it dear. I need someone to talk to when there is no one else around. When I can't find flesh, I need a Spirit to keep me sane, to keep me straight, to keep me from shooting myself; to keep me focused. I need that. I need it. That's the spark plug, the battery that fuels my life. I can't make it without Jesus, I'm telling you, and wouldn't want to make it without him.

"Urgency and Assurance of Salvation"

St. James AME Church Women's Retreat
"The Flavor of a Woman"
June 29 – July 1, 2007

We are living in a time when our very lifestyles are contrary to God's will. We condone all kinds of sexual immorality and other sins and call it tolerance or alternative lifestyle. We used to have the freedom to live without fear of drive-by shootings and armed robberies. Places that used to feel safe aren't safe anymore. Young people are being killed at parties, walking down the street, at the movies, and on the school grounds. More and more people are abusing alcohol trying to drown their problems. You can pour all the alcohol you want on your problems, but it won't drown them. Sexual sins, especially against our children, is out of hand and God is not pleased. Children are killing their parents, parents are killing their children, and I could go on and on. Our world appears more-full of trouble every day.

The Word of God warns us when it says "in the last days, perilous (troublesome) times shall come." (II Timothy 3:1)

We live in a fast technological age. Everything is pretty much operated by a machine or a computer. I mean, they have phones that can do more than I want them to do, cars talking to you . . . we are truly living in the fast lane. We want everything fast, quick, and in a hurry.

Be reminded, God is more concerned with the direction of our lives than He is with the speed at which we travel. If we don't slow down as a nation and change, we will destroy ourselves or be destroyed.

God says in II Chronicles 7:14, "If my people, who are called by my name, will humble themselves, and pray, and seek my face, and turn from their wicked ways, then will I hear from heaven and will forgive their sin and will heal their land."

There is urgency and a need for assurance.

Even if you are a joyous, optimistic woman, you may find your spirit almost broken by the inevitable disappointments and tragedies that are the inevitable consequences of righteous living. Singer Judy Collins observed, "Grief shows us the beauties of life and teaches us to appreciate them."

There is urgency and a need for assurance.

It is time to stop faking salvation and playing church. I know it's a fake because the church of God has power to change and make a difference in our communities. There are churches on every corner and in between. But the people who attend are just like the world – no power to change.

If we sincerely want to change ourselves for the better, we must start on the inside and work our way out. We must be born again. Lasting change doesn't occur "out there," it occurs "in here." It occurs, not in the shifting sands of our own particular circumstances, but in the quiet depths of our own hearts.

If you truly desire a new beginning or a new you, don't expect changing circumstances, changing churches, changing jobs, changing husbands or getting a husband, don't expect any of that to miraculously transform you into the person God wants you to be. Transformation starts with God and it starts in the silent center of a humble heart. You must experience the new birth.

You must love God, and you can't love God until you love Jesus. And Jesus said, "If you love me, keep my commandments." You will have to make a choice to follow Jesus. He said, "If any man will come after me, let him deny himself and take up his cross daily and follow me." Then you have to "seek first the kingdom of God."

Lean upon God's promises and accept the touch of His comforting hand. Remember that God rules both mountaintops and valleys. He does it with limitless wisdom and love now and forever.

There is urgency and a need for assurance of salvation.

I Corinthians 10:13 says, "There hath no temptation taken you but such as is common to man; but God is faithful who will not suffer you to be tempted above that ye are able, but will with the temptation also make a way to escape, that ye may be able to bear it."

God is faithful to us even when we are not faithful to Him. God keeps His promises. He offers us countless blessings, but He does not force His blessings upon us.

If we are to experience His love and His grace, we must claim them for ourselves. Talk with God often, seek His guidance, watch for His signs, listen to the wisdom that He shares through the reliable voice of His word. God loves you, and you deserve all the best that God has to offer.

How bright do you believe your future to be? What are you expecting? If you are not saved, you have a very dim and dismal future. You really don't have any hope. If you do have some hope, it's false.

I have a greater hope; my hope is in Jesus, the author and finisher of my faith. I don't have to worry about my future; I know who holds my future. Corrie Ten Boom had this advice – "Never be afraid to trust an unknown future to a known God."

God promised to never leave me. He told me to fear not, for He is always with me.

There is urgency and a need for assurance of salvation. I have my assurance. Do you have yours?

CHAPTER FIFTEEN
My Heart

Vindicate me, O Lord, for I have led a blameless life; I have trusted in the Lord without wavering. Test me, O Lord, and try me, examine my heart and my mind; for your love is ever before me, and I walk continually in your truth. I do not sit with deceitful men, nor do I consort with hypocrites;

Psalms 26:1-5 (NIV)

What have you liked best about your life so far?

The thing I like best about my life is that I am me. I thank God that I don't try to be anybody else. I don't try to impress anybody. I'm just me. I like being me and don't apologize for it.

What things are most important to you now?

The things of God, my family, and people in general are all important; however my family is most important to me. I love people. Everything else is going to pass away. God loves people. He cares about how we treat one another; how we get along. God made us and created us to be in communion with him and sin messed that up. Men fight with each other and God is not pleased with that.

Brothers and sisters are fighting over material things after the death of their loved ones. Families are dear to my heart, but God is first. That's why I want a ministry where I can help people solve their problems and help them to see what is important. Because when a person hurts your heart or a loved one dies, what can things do for you then? It doesn't matter how much your wedding ring cost and what your wedding dress was like if your child was killed. None of that matters.

Who do you trust and depend on?

The Lord Jesus Christ. I depend on Him and trust Him. Man says one thing but he may not be able to bring it to pass. Man may not be able to keep his word. When it comes to Jesus, He is faithful to His promises. He promised to never leave me nor forsake me, and He said that He would supply all of my needs. What else do I need? He even said that He would comfort me, that He would keep me in perfect peace if I keep my mind stayed on Him. Why would I trust somebody else? I don't trust my job, man, my children, my husband. You see, they are subject not to be there. My husband is going to leave me one day or I'm going to leave him. Death is going to take him or me. We don't have a choice. Even in death, God is with me. I depend on God.

When my emotions get involved, for example, when people mistreat me, it hurts. But I can't go after them and fuss. I try not to do that anymore, get upset. I can't remember the last time I was angry. That's not good for my physical being, let alone my spiritual being. I have gotten upset, emotionally crying, but not mad and angry with somebody to hurt them. No, I can't remember a time. I do get mad at the devil when I see what he's doing to people. I can't hit him, you can only tell him off with the Word of God. It is written, "Satan get behind me, leave me alone."

If you had the power to solve one problem in the world, what would it be and why?

I would solve hate and indifference with the love, care and compassion of Jesus Christ. I believe we could overcome any and everything if we loved people, loved one another. If someone I know needs food and I have some, I'm going to share. That includes clothing, money, etc. It wouldn't be a lack of anything in the world. The Word of God says love covers a multitude of sins, and what is sin based on...hate, pride, pride of life, flesh, material things, love of money. Love would cover all of that. Thank you, Lord Jesus.

How do you define a good life or successful life?

Be happy. If you are happy with what you're doing; you feel good about yourself; you can get up in the morning, grin and smile, that's it. Happiness doesn't come from things. It doesn't come from positions. It comes from agape love. It comes from logos, the Word of God. It comes from those kinds of things; things you can't touch. You know how you feel when you do something good to help somebody and you feel all good inside. When you can have that feeling all of the time or most of the time, you can't buy that. That's something that money can't buy. Thank God, because everybody doesn't have enough money to buy it.

Over time how have you looked at life and people?

I didn't pay people that much attention when I was young, but knew that I always cared for people. I was always thrust into a position of helping people and I didn't know that that was my heart and my love.

Over time, I have learned that life is not that serious. It's serious, but not that serious. Because it's in the hand of the Lord, I can loosen up, be free and enjoy it. People are here to be loved and love me, so we can enjoy each other. Over time, I have seen what God loves. God loves people, He does not love things. So if I love people, I can be happy because that's what God loves. God is love. Over time, I have seen how that is important. People are so important. It doesn't matter what they do. They can be murderers, rapists, molesters, but they are still people, and God still loves them. That's why I cannot look upon a person that has committed a crime as the worst criminal. I still look at them and see people. I still look at them and see somebody that is lost and doesn't know the Lord doesn't know how good he can be. They are going through struggles in life because they don't know where peace is. Peace is in Christ Jesus. It's not in the world. Peace won't be here until Jesus comes. I learned to love people more; accept people for who they are, but try to help them become all that they can be.

Judge Barbara H. Caldwell

Testimonials from men and women whose lives she has touched.

Although I have known Judge Barbara Caldwell and appeared before her for 20 years as Chief Assistant District Attorney for Douglas County, I did not really know her as I do now until the past few years. During that time God called me to a reborn and resurgent faith which opened my heart to see in her, what many have known for so long. Barbara Caldwell carries a Godly countenance about her life as both Judge and woman of wisdom, and compassion. She drives a white truck with a front license plate that simply says, "BLESSED." But it means also that all of us are blessed when we see her.

Beau McClain
Chief Assistant District Attorney

God does nothing without a purpose. When He put Barbara Caldwell in my life, it was for the purpose of teaching me how to deny myself, take up my cross, and follow Him daily. She is a woman of God, wife, mother, mentor, teacher, and a good friend who will tell you the truth about yourself with meekness according to God's

Word. I thank God for Sister Barbara. I could not have asked for a better example than the one God purposed in my life.

Virginia Williams
Accountant

I've had the honor of meeting Sister Caldwell through the Women in the Word Bible Study that she teaches. I was looking for a Bible Study at the time, and I know that God sent me to her. She has truly been a blessing in my life. She challenges me, making sure that I totally understand what a verse is saying before she moves on. She encourages me to make the Word the foundation of my life. I know that you should not follow man as your example in your walk with Christ, but I can truly say that if there were anyone I would want as an example, it would definitely be Sister Barbara Caldwell. She is a true example of letting your light shine before men!

Erica Kemp
Judicial Secretary

My first contact with Barbara Caldwell was at Mt. Zion Baptist Church where she taught the children in Sunday school. My children were privileged to develop a relationship with her before I did. They loved her class and often told me what she had taught them, which was a positive influence in their lives.

As time progressed, I was able to spend time with Sister Caldwell at various church functions, and we developed a great friendship. I learned to admire and appreciate her love for God and God's people, her zeal to be like Christ, and most of all her wisdom and knowledge of God's word. This made me want to spend more time in this Godly woman's presence, and I started to attend her weekly ladies' Bible study class. Through this time of study and prayer, I developed a loving, long lasting relationship with Sister Caldwell and other ladies from the church.

Barbara Caldwell stands boldly and proudly as a child of God, and I admire her for what she believes. When she gives me advice, it is solid advice straight from God's word. God has used her to be a positive influence in my life. She has been a true friend through the good and the bad, the ups and the downs. She has always been right there for me and for other women. What a friend indeed! Being who she is and loving me for who I am has influenced me to want to walk in her steps. She is truly a positive influence in my life. May she be blessed always!

Judy Robinson
Salesperson

If you ever have the privilege of meeting Barbara Caldwell, you will know as I do that she is a true woman of God. Her powerful presence, genuine manner, and warm personality are reflected in the many lives she has touched over the years. She exudes grace, strength, and brilliance. She has been recognized as a "first" in many of her numerous accomplishments and milestones. The public exclaims she was "the first Black," "the first woman," "the first in Georgia" in many of her accomplishments. It is no surprise to those who know her that she is a successful judge who has presided over a courtroom for over twenty years. Her judicial decisions are not made lightly. Good day or bad, rain or shine, she seeks God first before rendering her decisions. She teaches, preaches, praises, and blesses so many. She is always willing to lend her personal time, education, knowledge, and any available resources just to help those in need.

Judge Caldwell is a wife, daughter, mother, and grandmother who have through many trials, tribulations, and adversities held on. She always remains steadfast, non-shakable and non-wavering. If there existed a "Life Percentage Meter" to rank us for giving of ourselves, Barbara Caldwell's number would be 200%. I am privileged to call Barbara Caldwell my friend.

Carla Overshown-Wells

Real Estate Agent

JUSTICE ROBERT BENHAM

The 6th Annual Evening with the Advocates
Keynote Speaker

Justice Robert Benham began his judicial career on the Court of Appeals of Georgia where he served for six years beginning in 1984. In 1989, he was appointed to the Supreme Court of Georgia and served as Presiding Justice from 1994 to 1995. Justice Benham became Chief Justice in 1995 and held that position until 2001. He continues to serve on the Court having been reelected in 2002 to serve his third six-year term.

During Justice Benham's tenure as Chief Justice, the Supreme Court of Georgia was listed as one of the most progressive supreme courts in the nation by the *American*

Bar Association Journal. Additionally, Justice Benham was listed in *Georgia Trend* magazine as one of the 100 Most Influential Georgians for six years while serving as Chief Justice and is presently listed as a Notable Georgian. He was named by *Ebony* magazine as one of the 100 most influential blacks in America for three consecutive years during his term as Chief Justice of the Georgia Supreme Court.

Justice Benham was educated at Tuskegee University, the University of Georgia and the University of Virginia. He engaged in the private practice of law for fifteen years before entering the judiciary.

Justice Benham serves on the Board of Curators of the Georgia Historical Society, Board of Directors of the Georgia Preservation and Trust, the Westville Historical Society, the Noble-Hill Wheeler Historical Society and the Georgia Legal History Foundation. He is a past Master in the Bleckley Inns of Court and a member of the Georgia Chamber of Commerce. He has also served on the University of Georgia Foundation, as Chairman of the University of Georgia Law School Alumni Association, and on numerous other social, civic, professional, fraternal, and business organizations.

Justice Benham has been honored with many awards, including Distinguished Service Awards from the State

Bar of Georgia, Martin Luther King, Jr. Commission and the NAACP. He was the proud recipient of the 2004 Spirit of Scouting Award.

Justice Benham is a former member of the American Trial Lawyers Association, Georgia Trial Lawyers Association and Georgia Conference of Black Lawyers. He served on the Board of Directors of the Conference of Chief Justices and as United States Supreme Court Chief Justice William Rhenquist's appointee to the Federal-State Jurisdiction Committee. He currently serves on the Board of Directors of the Judicial Council of the National Bar Association and is the State of Georgia's liaison to the National Consortium on Racial and Ethnic Fairness in the Courts. Justice Benham has lectured at numerous law schools and served as facilitator for legal conferences in twenty-six states on topics ranging from judicial administration to appellate practice.

In the legal arena, he was instrumental in creating Georgia's Indigent Defense Program, and he received national, state and local awards for creating Georgia's first Drug Courts. The State Bar of Georgia Community Service Award is named after Justice Benham, as well as the first Law Camp for High School students. He received the Distinguished Public Service Award from the Litigation Section of the Atlanta Bar Association and the 2007 R. Prudence Herndon Award from the Gate City Bar

Association. He recently received the 2007 William Hastie Award from the National Bar Association at its national meeting held in Atlanta. Justice Benham created Georgia's first Comprehensive Legal Education Program which has allowed over 200 minority students to attend law school.

Justice Benham has received numerous awards and recognitions for his involvement with the business community. His family has been involved in various types of businesses from 1880 to the present. He is a lifetime member of the Cartersville-Bartow Chamber of Commerce, and he is a member of the Georgia Chamber of Commerce. Recently, Justice Benham received the first Ethics Advocacy Award from the Southern Center for Ethics and Professionalism where he serves on the Board of Directors. Justice Benham has served as Chairman of the Coosa Valley Area Planning and Development Commission, Bartow County Development Authority and he serves as the Georgia Supreme Court liaison for the Fulton County Business Court. He was the 2005 recipient of the J. W. Fanning Award from the Leadership Georgia Foundation. He has received the National Pharmacy Award of Achievement, National Alumni Award from the University of Georgia, National Trumpet Award which salutes African American Achievement, the Alumni Outstanding Service Award from Tuskegee University, and the Outstanding Service and Contribution Award from the National Association of Blacks in Criminal Justice.

Justice Benham is a member of the Deacons Board of the Greater Mt. Olive Baptist Church and he is a member of the Eta Lambda Chapter of Alpha Phi Alpha and a member of Kappa Boule. He is a Mason, Shriner and Elk. Justice Benham is married to the former Nell Dodson and they have two children, Corey and Austin, and four grandchildren.

About the Authors

Frederick D. Jones is a Business Law & Ethics Lecturer at Kennesaw State University in Kennesaw, Georgia, practicing attorney, and Christian author. An ordained Minister since 1999, Mr. Jones founded *The Advocates of Christ, Inc.* in Baton Rouge, Louisiana. This ministry is dedicated to promoting the practice of integrity and character with spiritual excellence in the legal and business professions. As founder of *The Advocates Association, LLC*, an educational consulting firm targeting community service entities; this ministry is committed to serving, covering and supporting churches, ministries and non-profits. Mr. Jones is dedicated to strengthening the structure of all service and faith based organizations such that the message of Jesus Christ may continue to go forth in complete legal compliance with the law. Moreover his life mission and passion is to improve the quality of justice by merging law and ministry. Fred and his two sons, Freddie and Jonathan currently reside in Marietta, Georgia.

ALL RISE!

Kennesaw State UNIVERSITY

Office of the President

May 4, 2006

Dr. Frederick D. Jones
Accounting
Mailbox #0402
CAMPUS

Dear Frederick:

What a marvelous talk you gave at the "Celebration of Commitment" between Kennesaw State University and Zion Baptist Church on April 23rd. Indeed, you were eloquent, provocative, insightful, and humorous all in one speech. Obviously, you are a masterful teacher/preacher/lawyer, and I came away mesmerized by your ability to capture an audience's attention, as well as grateful that you are a member of the KSU community. You do us proud!

I was so pleased that you could represent us on this important occasion in the life of the church and the college. Our institutions have been partners in social stewardship for years now, and it has always been one of my most cherished duties as president to bring greetings from Kennesaw State to Reverend Travis and the church family. Even though this will be my last formal "Zion Day" as president of KSU, I plan to continue my relationship with the church in whatever way I can. It has long been a place of my heart.

Again, Frederick, please know how tremendously impressed I was with your excellent talk. Keep up your great work!

My warm personal regards and best wishes.

Sincerely,

Betty L. Siegel
President

BLS:jbw

1000 Chastain Rd. • #0101 • Kennesaw Hall • Bldg. 1, Rm. 5600 • Kennesaw, GA 30144-5591

Phone: (770)423-6033 • Fax: (770) 423-6543 • www.kennesaw.edu

Lucinda Perry is a civil rights attorney and author in Douglas County Georgia. She serves The Advocates of Christ Ministries in the capacity as Director of Membership. Visit Lucinda at:
www.LucindaForYourRights.com

"...and who knows but that you have come to royal position for such a time as this?" Esther 4:14

OUR HISTORY

In the spring of 1992, several Southern University Law School students expressed a need for encouragement and support for those who openly professed a belief in Jesus Christ. This expression of interest and need resulted in the formation of a fellowship group which was later named the Advocates of Christ a/k/a "The Advocates."

This group consisted of students from a broad diversity of church traditions committed to the singular purpose of communicating the message of Jesus Christ through their personal lives.

Today, many of the founding Advocates are in various states continuing the vision of serving Jesus Christ through the practice of law.

OUR PURPOSE

Serve, cover, and support pastors, the local church, and the five-fold ministry by offering consulting educational services designed to structure, strengthen and bring into legal compliance the foundational business aspects of ministry.

OUR MISSION

Reaching judges, attorneys, legal professionals and students for the cause of Jesus Christ

OUR VISION

To raise up a family and community of Advocates who are passionately and practically demonstrating the love of Jesus and merging the practice of law and ministry by practicing integrity and demonstrating character. I see a community of judges and attorneys dedicated to serving, supporting, structuring, and covering the local church, ministries and non-profits such that we may ensure that the gospel of Jesus Christ continues to go forth uninhibited and in legal compliance with the laws around the world. I see judges, attorneys, pastors, ministers working side by side carrying out the Great Commission of spreading the gospel of Jesus Christ. I see all Advocates engaging in activities to improve the law, the legal system and the administration of justice. I see churches cancelling crime in their communities by demonstrating the gospel and working in harmony with the legal system.

OUR CORE VALUES

Character, Courage, Philanthropy, Honesty, Fellowship, Friendship, Confidentiality, Faith, Family, Attitude, Health, Finance, Growth, Loyalty, and Love

OUR MOTTO

We are practicing the principles of integrity and character with spiritual excellence.

OUR ACTIVITIES

- Professional fellowship with a spiritual focus
- Recognition of outstanding service
- Celebration of achievement
- Advancement of positive community initiatives
- Publication of life changing life stories
- Consulting pastors and ministry leaders
- Resourceful associations and affiliations

www.advocatesofchrist.org

"PRACTICING INTEGRITY AND CHARACTER WITH SPIRITUAL EXCELLENCE"

Valerie Adams, Esq., GA

Jenohn L. Smith, Esq., KY

Audrey Arrington, Esq., GA

Stephone Johnson, Esq., GA

Sandra Clarke, Esq., GA

Michael Jones, Esq., GA

LaDonna Collier, Esq., NY

A. J. Mitchell, Esq., GA

LaShonda Council, Esq., GA

Lesa Pamplin, Esq., TX

Mawuli Davis, Esq., GA

Lucinda Perry, Esq., GA

Michel L. Davis, Esq., GA

David Rachel, Esq., GA

Terence P. Malloy, Esq., GA

Margaret Edwards, Esq., LA

Verna Ross, Esq., CA

Traci D. Ellis, Esq., GA

Dawn Scotland, Esq., GA

Shera Grant, Esq., GA

Vonia Shields-Fleet, Esq., LA

Zebie Grayson, Esq., LA.

Marisha Steward, Esq., GA

Latonia P. Hines, Esq., GA

Otis L. Weldon, Esq., GA

Louise T. Hornsby, Esq., GA

Rhonda Wesley, Esq., MO

Kevin James, Esq., LA

Michelle West, Esq., GA

Frederick D. Jones, Esq., LA